SERVE:

Others First In a Me-First World

C O U R T N E Y   R E E S

WESTBOW
PRESS
A DIVISION OF THOMAS NELSON

WestBow Press books may be ordered through booksellers or by contacting:

WestBow Press
A Division of Thomas Nelson
1663 Liberty Drive
Bloomington, IN 47403
www.westbowpress.com
1-(866) 928-1240

Photo by Kyle Heaser of Lead Image Photography
http://leadimagephotography.com

Scriptures taken from the Holy Bible, New International Version®, NIV®. Copyright © 1973, 1978, 1984, 2011 by Biblica, Inc.™ Used by permission of Zondervan. All rights reserved worldwide. www.zondervan.com The "NIV" and "New International Version" are trademarks registered in the United States Patent and Trademark Office by Biblica, Inc.™
All rights reserved.

ISBN: 978-1-4908-0736-2 (sc)
ISBN: 978-1-4908-0735-5 (hc)
ISBN: 978-1-4908-0737-9 (e)

Library of Congress Control Number: 2013915998

Printed in the United States of America.

WestBow Press rev. date: 09/03/2013

FOREWORD

I vividly remember the meeting where our team had to pray about and discuss the core actions of GT Church. We came to the understanding that vision answers the "what" of our action and values answers the "how" of our action, but if theory doesn't lead to specific action, it will not lead to life transformation. Therefore, we knew that we had to determine what actions we would put in place to breathe life into our vision.

In that meeting, we wrote SERVE down the left side of the board and began to discuss a word and phrase for each letter. That prayerful discussion led to a shared set of values that gave birth to a culture that has started an avalanche of ministry in our church and community. SERVE: Others First in a "Me First" World will unpack each aspect of the SERVE vision and will hopefully open your heart to a clearer revelation of God's call on your life and the life of your church.

S—Share One Vision
E—Embrace Excellence
R—Recruit Others
V—Value People
E—Experience Growth

This acrostic along with each letter's definition will serve as the chapters that lie ahead of you in this book. I remember reading Luke 10 and realizing that every aspect of our SERVE values were found, defined, and illustrated in those forty-two verses. Therefore, Luke 10 will serve as a large part of the biblical context for this book.

As I dug deeper into Luke 10, I began to see that Luke seems to ask four questions of every follower of Jesus Christ:

What makes you serve? (Luke 10:1–16) We are very familiar with the apostles Peter, James, and John. From there, it can get a little more difficult for some of us to remember. Luke gives all their names in Luke 6:12–16.

> One of those days Jesus went out to a mountainside to pray, and spent the night praying to God. When morning came, he called his disciples to him and chose twelve of them, whom he also designated apostles: Simon (whom he named Peter), his brother Andrew, James, John, Philip, Bartholomew, Matthew, Thomas, James son of Alphaeus, Simon who was called the Zealot, Judas son of James, and Judas Iscariot, who became a traitor.

In Luke 10, we come to understand that Jesus was not limited to just the twelve: seventy-two others obeyed His call and helped Jesus spread the gospel. I'm intrigued by the personalities of those seventy-two servants and their passion for serving Christ. Luke 9 tells us that the harvest is plentiful, but the laborers are still few.

What makes you rejoice? (Luke 10:17–24) The disciples were excited that demons were being cast out and were obeying them when they used Jesus' name, but Jesus reminded them that what should cause them to rejoice was that their names were written in heaven. Ministry is more about opportunity and responsibility than mere authority and power.

What makes you pause? (Luke 10:25–37) We can discuss serving in the abstract, but when we actually engage people in ministry and service, it will cost us something. Serving costs us time, energy, and oftentimes our finances. The challenge for us is this: Do we pause when we see injustice and hurt, or like the priest and Levite, do we look for an escape? We are never more Christlike than when we feel a person's pain and seek to help.

What makes you listen? (Luke 10:38–42) I personally believe that listening to Jesus should be the basis for all serving. Experiencing Christ should translate into spiritual growth, and that can never be separated from serving others. Spending time with Jesus and hearing His Word is critical if we really want to make an impact by serving others. Doing so reminds us that in a "me first" world, at the end of the day it needs to be Christ first.

One of the greatest aspects of this SERVE project has been the privilege of working with such a great team, particularly Courtney Rees. I cannot think of a person with more qualifications to help write such a book on serving in the context of GT Church. I say that not only because Courtney was an outstanding student as an English major at Vanguard University but also because I have watched her grow up physically and spiritually at GT and serve in so many critical areas of ministry in the church, including on our church staff. Talent runs deep in the Rees family, as Courtney's sister Britney created all of the amazing illustrations that you see in this book. I know I share in the gratitude that their parents, Tom and Sherry Rees, must have toward Christ as they see how God is using their daughters!

My prayer is that this book will impact everyone who reads it by deepening his or her desire to know Christ and make Him known. May the pages that follow add some helpful insight and inspiration to the ongoing conversation in your heart and personal ministry as to what it means to serve others and Jesus Christ.

—Bryan D. Koch,
Lead Pastor, GT Church

share one vision

Conversations in the Air

Rare, beautiful conversations have taken place for me while seated next to a stranger on an airplane. There was the pastor with an extraordinary love story. The college student who became deathly ill from a poisonous spider bite. The artist whose story of redemption moved me to tears. These airplane conversations were glimpses into their lives, teaching me something from their stories.

Conversing with a stranger positioned forty thousand feet above the ground has an unearthly sense to it. There is clarity within a lively tête-à-tête with an unknown person. It is unclouded by longstanding

1

impressions or personal history. Situated on an airplane, all contextual nuances are removed. Besides the slight deviances of first class and coach, we are each found in the same framework—people in transition, suspended between two destinations. Time freezes as we are up there conversing, allotting an elevated dose of perspective from the harried worlds we have escaped from if even for only a few hours.

Perhaps we find freedom in knowing that our interactions in the sky have a definitive start and finish, from liftoff to landing. The knowledge of the inevitable parting at baggage claim eliminates some of the relational walls we claim to be "normal." We have no commitments to uphold or intimacy to further—just truthfulness in conversation. In those starkly truthful conversations, I have observed an undeniable fact: Human beings, as a whole, have uncanny similarities to one another. Although we may style our hair differently, work different jobs, and maintain different definitions of what family and home look like, we all have basic desires. We all have been in and out of love. We all face fear, insecurity, and failure. We all have something that brings us to life and makes us feel more alive. We all hope, worry, strive, eat, sit, and think.

My conversation with Anne enlivened the truth about our universal similarities. We were both flying to California, and at a quick glance, we were nothing alike. I was flying to a friend's wedding. Anne was headed to a family reunion. We both had long hair, mine wavy and brown, hers stick-straight and raven black with streaks of gray fighting to surface. During the hour-and-a-half flight, her story tumbled out.

Anne's Story

Anne grew up in the heart of New York City, and even as a child, she was eager to experience the world of the arts. Luckily, beauty and talent took a liking to her as well. As a young adult, she landed a role on Broadway in the opening season of Godspell. She talked about her early years on Broadway with a faint glow. She explained that there was not a great sense of community on Broadway at the time, and despite her success, she was unhappy.

"As a good Jewish girl, I was never taught about Jesus growing up, but I grew to respect Him from being in Godspell," she went on. "You see, although I had 'made it' by most people's standards, I still felt like I was missing something in my life." After about a year into the show, Jesus caught her attention when the man playing the role of Jesus said the line from Scripture verbatim, "Love your neighbor as yourself."[1] One night during the performance, those words hit her. She didn't know how she had missed it before! Anne then knew what she had been missing: She was not loving people enough.

Anne's realization carved the path for the next year of her life. She quit Broadway, packed her stuff into an RV, and traveled the United States. She visited charities and community organizations and stopped at diners, churches, and spiritual centers. She was soul-searching and people-watching. She interacted with people and watched how they interacted with each other.

"I noticed that a lot of people really did care about others," Anne said. She decided she would help anybody who needed it and was sincere. "But I was stunned by how many more did not seem to love or care for anyone beside themselves," she said with conviction. She wondered what was stopping these people from living to their full potential. What was preventing them from loving others?

These conclusions altered Anne's outlook on life. She devoted herself to living unselfishly. She adjusted her worldview and engaged herself in organizations that revolved around helping others. Throughout the remainder of our conversation, she shared the many ways she strives to live a life devoted to helping others.

Anne reminded me that human beings crave community and

---

1   Mark 12:31

long for a grander purpose beyond themselves. As C. S. Lewis describes in his book Mere Christianity, we all are configured to know the difference between right and wrong, good and evil. We all lean toward favoring the person who makes a sacrifice. We all respect unselfishness, even if we do not display it. We innately know it is the best way to be. Malachi 3:18 states, "And you will again see the distinction between the righteous and the wicked, between those who serve God and those who do not." Right and wrong, selfish or not, we all know how we should behave, even outside of the Christian faith.

After my conversation with Anne, I was startled by the thought that she was following Jesus' teaching without actually believing Him to be the Son of God. She followed Jesus' words, not out of moral obligation or a commitment to follow the path of Christianity, but simply because it is what made sense. Yet many of us, who call ourselves Christians, do not live unselfishly.

In a very large way, we are missing what Anne has mastered. Her life resembles that of Christ's more than many Christians' lives. Anne's life told a story, and it was a story bigger than her own self-preoccupations. It was a story about serving.

Storyboard

In college, I studied a wide range of topics—literature, writing techniques, plays, poetry—but we never engaged in a lot of conversation about filmmaking. This was unfortunate since, immediately following college, the church hired me to write video scripts. It was most unfortunate for my friend Andrew, the videographer. Our meetings normally played out as follows: I would write a script, and he would shoot the footage. We would copy and paste our portions together, add music, and the finished short film would emerge. It was a mishmashed attempt at collaboration, for we were both disappointed with the final outcome. The problem was not in our skill levels but in our misaligned vision. Although each of us could envision the video individually, we were lacking a translation. We needed a new method.

In the world of film, a storyboard is the premiere preproduction, pre-visualization tool designed to give a frame-by-frame, shot-by-shot script...to organize all the complicated action.[2]

A storyboard sounded like a good idea to me. I presented my storyboarded script to Andrew, and we were off. We worked side by side, tweaking the words, choosing the shots, and by its completion, we were both proud of the final outcome. What made the difference between the written script and the storyboard?

The storyboard helped us to share the same vision. It painted a preliminary picture of where we were headed, and once we understood the vision, our end product was a tangible display of our joint effectiveness.

Combined efforts are always most effective. Have you ever been part of a team that disagreed on vision? It's mayhem. It's like the crew of a ship trying to navigate without agreeing on a destination. Most times, you end up somewhere that you didn't intend to go, such as Greenland or Trumpet Island. As with any team or organization, it is important that churches agree on their vision.

When I worked at Glad Tidings, our creative planning team would dream up themes and ideas for the weekend services. Despite assumptions about church-life dynamics, our meetings did not always end agreeably. We would disagree about service order, creative elements, and song choices. Yet I learned that all of these small discrepancies were inconsequential. Why? Because we understood the vision. At the end of the day, as long as we were clinging to our vision,

---

2   John Hart, *The Art of the Storyboard: A Filmmaker's Introduction* (Amsterdam: Elsevier/Focal Press, 2008).

everything else was secondary. Details are important; they are the magnifying glass that illuminates excellence, but the vision is the compass. The vision is due north. It is the overarching reminder that as long as we are getting that one thing right, we are doing okay.

Every church has a unique vision with a mission statement catered to their culture, community, and language. Church visions can sound different and look different, but essentially, they should all capture the message of the Gospels in some fashion. In the same way that people have different personalities, so do churches. In that sense, church visions will differ slightly, but we are all working collectively for the same cause. A letter to the Corinthians emphasizes this: "There are different kinds of service, but the same Lord. There are different kinds of working, but in all of them and in everyone it is the same God at work" (1 Cor. 12:5–6). At Glad Tidings, our church vision is "helping people become fully devoted followers of Jesus Christ." Whatever yours is, the vision is the guiding force behind the church community.

"Having a clear vision statement provides a tremendous sense of unity and freedom because everyone understands what they are trying to accomplish and who they are trying to reach."[3] Jesus' vision is the unifying force that binds together each eclectic movement of believers. Therefore, in order to wholly live and love as Jesus did, it is important to understand His vision. Why did He come to Earth, and what was His primary purpose?

There is a story in the Gospels where Jesus wants to reveal His

---

3   Beach, Nancy. An Hour on Sunday: Creating Moments of Transformation and Wonder (Grand Rapids, MI: Zondervan, 2004).

vision to the disciples. He must have known that it wouldn't be effective enough with words alone, so He gave them a visual to assure that they could grasp His vision. He equally combined words and pictures and essentially storyboarded His vision through this beautiful visual documentary.

Tales of a Foot Washer

The disciples had traveled far. Layers of dust and grime coated their bodies and feet. Leather sandals protected them from cuts and sores but did little to barricade against sweat and soil. Perhaps even worse than the dirty appearance was the lingering stench, indicating a long journey. The twelve men and their leader, all suffering from tired feet and physical exhaustion, sat down to dinner. As the meal was set before them, Jesus stood up and wrapped a towel around His waist. The disciples looked at Him curiously as He picked up a basin and began filling it midway with water. He then acted in the most unexpected of ways as He lowered Himself to His knees. He looked at the first person at the table, Matthew, with loving, penetrating eyes and set the basin before him. He then began to wash Matthew's feet. The room was silent. The moment was sacred.

He moved to the next person seated at the table, Luke. Jesus' soft eyes connected with His disciple. Jesus studied the feet before Him as he carefully scrubbed all residue from the worn feet. The calloused feet were washed by the hands of a carpenter, the hands of a King.

Next He came to Peter. As Jesus knelt before him, the Savior lowering Himself to the stance of a servant, Peter felt uneasy. His mind was churning with the paradox demonstrated before him. Biting his tongue no longer, Peter broke the sacred silence again with a rebuttal, "No, you shall never wash my feet."[4] Peter was appalled that the Messiah would stoop to the role of servant. But Jesus did not

---

4   John 13:8

reconsider. Instead, He replied, "Unless I wash you, you have no part with me."[5]

Jesus was not merely offering to clean feet. Jesus was offering an invitation of oneness. He was inviting each person in that room into relationship with Him, as He submitted to them through a great act of love and service. Ultimately, through Jesus' answer, He was assuring Peter and the other disciples that the kingship He desired was not one of hierarchy but rather one of relationship. One of unity. He wanted Peter to latch onto the vision that He was demonstrating by means of a washbasin and a rag.

Later in the evening, when Jesus rose to take His place at the table once the feet of each of His followers had been thoroughly washed, He gave further explanation. Looking at each face around the table, He set the question before them, "Do you understand what I have done for you? …You call me 'Teacher' and 'Lord,' and rightly so, for that is what I am. Now that I, your Lord and Teacher have washed your feet, you also should wash one another's feet"[6]

Tag

What a vibrant story about a remarkable vision! When I envision a king, my mind bids a throne, a crown, elaborate dress, and decorum. But Jesus displays a man bending down with a washbasin in the garb of a slave. The magnitude of His action is striking. A king who came to serve. It is a great display of His confidence and His love for us.

Do you know what I hear Jesus saying to the disciples in this scene's last words? "Tag. You're it." They sit down to dinner, Jesus performs an outlandish act of love, and then He says, "Tag. It's your turn now." Jesus knew that He was not going to be around much longer with skin on, so He made sure that they understood His vision

---

5   John 13:8

6   John 13:14

and then said, "You also should ..." Serving was the legacy that Jesus chose to leave with His disciples.

There is a chapter in Luke that is wholly devoted to the idea of service. It begins with Jesus recruiting a large number of volunteers to spread into the surrounding communities to serve. The disciple who documented the stories in this gospel was the apostle Luke, who was a doctor (Col. 4:14). Luke was an intellectual who had an extensive vocabulary, especially with medical and nautical terms, and therefore, his gospel is written with precision and an acute attention to detail. When Luke describes Jesus' recruitment of the volunteers, he details the story with the number of seventy-two volunteers. In the first century, the religious leaders believed there to be seventy languages of the world (Genesis 10), so when Jesus sends out seventy, it is indicating that His message is for all languages and all people. Jesus says to the seventy workers, "He who listens to you listens to me; he who rejects you rejects me; but he who rejects me rejects him who sent me."[7] It is similar to what Jesus said to His disciples after washing their feet. On multiple occasions, He is laying out the framework for service and then saying, "There is no hierarchy here. Everyone is going to serve, including me. So tag. You're it." Jesus wants us to capture His vision and live accordingly.

Remember when the disciples asked Jesus how to pray and He led them in the Lord's Prayer? It starts out, "Our Father in heaven, hallowed be your name. Your Kingdom come, your will be done, on earth as it is in heaven." Jesus is teaching that the spiritual realm and the earthly realm are connected. He is the Son of God, but He still gave His life as a ransom. We are His beloved children, who are to also give our life as a ransom. Jesus does not ask us to do anything that He has not already accomplished Himself. And He said, "Tag. You're it ...On earth, as it is in heaven." It's a chain reaction. A domino effect. When you consider it, Jesus is giving us a huge level of responsibility.

7　Luke 10:16

He is nominating each of us to be models of Himself. It's a beautiful cacophony of the melding of heaven and earth with one unified message about love and service.

Vision-doers

The word vision can be annoying. I'll be honest. Sometimes when businesses and corporations talk about vision, I mentally check out. Oftentimes the word vision is code for empty rhetoric that captures ideas that never become a reality.

In my college years, our freshmen class was promised the grandiosity of what was titled, "Vision 2010." By the year of our graduation, we would supposedly witness glittering renovations and new structures. The spokespersons for the project made it sound marvelous. However, the four years succeeding these lofty promises were filled with financial struggles and staffing changes within the school. Consequentially, Vision 2010 was a flop. I think on my alma mater affectionately, which is why I could make light of it through our senior prank. Dodging campus security under the guise of night, our midnight caper was the spray-painted words Vision 2010 spread proudly across the front lawn of the campus. It was a teasing nod to the administration that they shouldn't make promises they can't keep.

Vision can be exhilarating and fun to dream about, but it only has value when it materializes into reality. A vision was never intended to exist as fancy words filling up a tab on a website. Unfortunately, I think Christians can create a bad rep for themselves because they function like Vision 2010—good intentions and lofty plans that never come to fruition. We are vision-sayers but not always vision-doers. The definition of vision is "the faculty of sight."[8] Essentially, vision is the blueprint stage. Yet once we have seen, we must also act. We must erect the vision. As stated in James 1:23–25,

> Anyone who listens to the word but does not do what it says is like someone who looks at his face in a mirror, and after looking at himself, goes away and immediately forgets what he looks like. But whoever looks intently into the perfect law that gives freedom, and continues in it—not forgetting what they have heard, but doing it—they will be blessed in what they do.

If we are aware of Christ's vision yet walk away from it as though we are still unaware, our lives will continue in discontented emptiness. I guarantee it. There are other visions that we can surely grasp hold of that will sustain us and motivate us for a spell, but they are temporal.

Vision can only be effective if we choose to let it guide us unquestionably through the path of our life, infiltrating itself into our decisions, choices, and investments. If the entire body of Christ shared the same vision and acted on it, we would be an unstoppable force! A vast community of believers solely devoted to living unabashedly for God and for others through our service. It would be astonishing.

Love Challenge

I read about a challenge that asked you to substitute the word love for serve for just one week. Instead of saying, "I love you" to your spouse, substitute "I serve you." Notice how it changes the weight of the

---

8   The American Heritage Dictionary of the English Language, 5th ed. (Boston, MA: Houghton Mifflin Harcourt Trade, 2011), s.v. "Vision," definition 1.

statement entirely. Suddenly, love is no longer butterflies and rainbows or that warm, fuzzy feeling. Now it has weight. It is a hard-earned love manifested through action. Perhaps this exact substitution is why Jesus hung so heavily on the idea of service. Jesus must have known that we would moderate the word love with passivity. We would disguise it with flowers and chocolate and think we had accomplished our task. In fact, we would even find pride in our love—turning it into self-promoting efforts for praise. The word serve, however, has less chance of becoming misconstrued. It is less likely to become a mere ideology. It's a hard-core action word.

Jesus chose to love the world by serving the world. You see, He made the two words interchangeable. He humbled Himself in service to demonstrate His love. His vision for serving people propelled His entire ministry and spoke love louder than anyone could have fathomed possible.

The Church

Once we understand our vision as Christ-followers, which is to simultaneously love and serve others, how can we accomplish this as a church body? When we are rushing from ministry event to ministry event—setting up, tearing down, cooking, cleaning, creating, administrating—amidst the hustle of a Sunday morning, it is not hard to lose sight of the vision.

What does vision do for a church, and why is it essential to cling to it? The importance of vision in the church is like the importance of a coach on a sports team. Although the coach is not a field player, he weaves together the framework for the entire game. He creates strategy. The coach makes it happen. In the same way, vision provides inspiration and framework for a church. Vision is the underlying message that announces, "There is a purpose for what you are doing, and it is much grander than the task you see before you." Vision is important, especially to those who serve behind the scenes at a church.

Oftentimes, we have a misguided perception that those who sing, preach, and teach are at the top of the SERVE ranking system. We imagine a hierarchy where the more a volunteer is behind the scenes the less is his or her significance. However, Jesus removed the ranking system, and vision sets the framework.

A couple at the church, Rick and Pauline, headed up our guest services team at the church that handles duties like greeting, handing out bulletins, collecting the offering, and distributing communion. They are also the troubleshooters who stand at the desk in the center of the atrium, ready for any problem or question that might come their way. Rick and Pauline invited me to one of their team meetings as a staff member presence, and I will never forget the way they spoke to their team. They started by cheering on their volunteers with words of encouragement and energy. They reminded their volunteers that they were not simply handing out bulletins with information or giving a mechanical hello. Stationed at the front doors of the church, they were inviting people into community and a message of hope simply through a warm smile and a kind demeanor. They were creating a welcoming presence. Essentially, Rick and Pauline were reminding their volunteers that they were helping people become fully devoted followers of Jesus Christ through the ways that they served. Vision puts service in perspective by inspiring us and laying down a framework.

Another facet of vision in the church is that it unifies people, and in that unity, it invigorates the prayers of the people. When we are reminded of vision, we are reminded that we are all working toward the same goal. Unfortunately, the church is not always defined as a place of congruency and harmony. Wherever there are people, there will be politics because people bring with them differences of opinion, motives, and agendas. It's inevitable. Vision is the common denominator, which helps us to rise above our differences. In that sense, it provides a unity to our prayer life as well. Phillip Yancey writes,

Prayer, and only prayer, restores my vision to one that more resembles God's. I awake from blindness to see that wealth lurks as a terrible danger, not a goal worth striving for; that value depends not on race or status but on the image of God every person bears; that no amount of effort to improve physical beauty has much relevance for the world beyond.[9]

The last essential of vision in a church is that it provides a purpose and reason for serving. Sometimes I love serving, but other times it feels like the lowest form of drudgery. I've heard people say that God doesn't ask much of us; however, I strongly disagree. I think God asks for everything, starting with the most intimate matters involving our heart and our motives. Within the church, we can perform tasks to the point of burnout, exhaustion, or completion, but unless our heart is engaged, we might as well not bother at all.

I love the story about Brother Lawrence, a French monk from the sixteenth century. He entered a monastery, assuming that he would spend his days in worship through prayer and holy tasks, so he was surprised when he was assigned to the kitchen staff. However, his time in the kitchen taught him more truths about God than could ever have been learned in a stained-glass setting. Brother Lawrence shared his thoughts,

> Nor is it needful that we should have great things to do ... We can do little things for God; I turn the cake that is frying on the pan for love of him, and that done, if there is nothing else to call me, I prostrate myself in worship before him, who has given me grace to work; afterwards

---

9   Philip Yancey, *Prayer: Does It Make Any Difference?* (Grand Rapids, MI: Zondervan, 2006).

I rise happier than a king. It is enough for me to pick up but a straw from the ground for the love of God.[10]

What I hear in that statement is a man who had a vision. When a person has vision, when a church has vision, every task has a greater purpose and a longer shelf life—eternity.

Share One Vision

Sharing one vision adds vigor and life to the church. It is an essential to the health of a church. But vision does not always flow naturally from our work as volunteers and church leaders. Maintaining vision is an intentional decision that must be continually sought. Here are several ways that a church can keep a clear focus while honing in on their vision.

1. Consistently Communicating the Vision

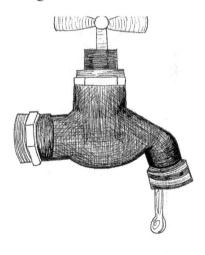

Bill Hybels from Willow Creek often says, "Vision leaks."[11] Have you ever had a vision that leaked? Perhaps you were working on a project that started out strong but lost steam. Or better yet, you had a New Year's resolution like "lose ten pounds" or "run every day." You begin invigorated, but with the passing of time, your vision dwindles and you lose motivation. Essentially, life

---

10   Mark Galli and Ted Olsen, 131 Christians Everyone Should Know (Nashville, TN: Broadman & Holman, 2000).

11   Beach, Nancy. An Hour on Sunday: Creating Moments of Transformation and Wonder (Grand Rapids, MI: Zondervan, 2004).

happens and time corrodes the clear vision you had on January first. The same happens within the church. If you forget about the vision, it begins to leak.

Many churches dedicate one weekend in the year to vision; it is like the church's new year. "Vision Sunday," or whatever your church titles it, is a day that hones in on church vision. It commemorates the church's history. It remembers the wins and losses and worships God for His faithfulness through the years. And then it casts vision. The problem is not with Vision Sunday but when a church only talks about their vision on one Sunday of the year. Vision must be consistently verbalized in order for it to be effective. Nancy Beach writes of leading volunteer teams, "It is essential for leaders of artists to err on the side of overcommunicating the purpose for serving and the church mission rather than assuming everyone just gets it and will always get it."[12] Volunteer meetings, life groups, the Sunday school classrooms, the pulpit— these can all be opportunities to cast vision. Some churches have retreats for their volunteers. Write the vision on literature that gets in the hands of everyone at the church to ensure that the vision is clear.

You'll notice Jesus was constantly restating His mission. Although He would frame it within various contexts, environments, and parables, He was always repeating the same message. It would have been difficult to spend a day with Jesus and walk away not knowing His vision.

I admire how Jesus could turn any situation into an opportunity to share His vision. One of my favorite examples of this occurs in Mark 10:33. Predicting His death once more, Jesus explains, "And the Son of Man will be betrayed to the chief priests and teachers of the law. They will condemn him to death and will hand him over to the Gentiles." The scene immediately follows with an abrupt discourse between

---

12   Beach, Nancy. An Hour on Sunday: Creating Moments of Transformation and Wonder (Grand Rapids, MI: Zondervan, 2004).

James and John when they say to Jesus, "We want you to do for us whatever we ask" (Mark 10:35). To me, this request sounds like the screech of brakes on pavement. It is hard to decipher if there was something lost in translation for James and John. Did they have selective hearing? Were they idiots? What was going on here? We hear Jesus acknowledge His approaching death for the sake of mankind, and then we hear James and John commence with a ridiculously self-centered request: "Let one of us sit at your right and the other at your left in your glory" (Mark 10:37). It sounds incredibly offensive within the context. But the request is also so fundamentally human.

As much as we might be tempted to judge their stupidity, we could just as easily hold up a mirror and hear ourselves echo the same naive request. Jesus says, "I will lay down my life for you." And we respond with "But what about us?" Jesus recognizes an opportunity to share His vision, and He capitalizes on the moment.

"You don't know what you are asking," Jesus said. "Can you drink the cup I drink or be baptized with the baptism I am baptized with? "We can," they answered.[13]

> Jesus said to them, "You will drink the cup I drink and
> be baptized with the baptism I am baptized with ...
> You know that those who are regarded as rulers of the
> Gentiles lord it over them, and their high officials exercise
> authority over them. Not so with you. Instead, whoever
> wants to become great among you must be your servant,
> and whoever wants to be first must be slave of all." (Mark
> 10:39–44)

He is explaining servant leadership, a new and peculiar concept. He is advocating an upside-down mind-set, a reverse ideology. He is explaining that the kingdom functions completely "other" than its

---

13 Mark 10:38-39

earthly counterparts. And then Jesus concludes with the verse that Pastor Bryan considers as the most important verse in the Bible. "For even the Son of Man did not come to be served, but to serve, and to give his life as a ransom for many" (Mark 10:45).

We have unique insight into this passage by knowing that James and John were martyred. They did not initially comprehend what Jesus meant by "the cup I drink." It sounds like it was a cup for the taking; however, Jesus is referring to the cup of blood, the communion cup, and, ultimately, the cup of suffering. It is not until much later, when James is crucified and John is tortured, that we see this story come full circle. The metaphorical cup of suffering was consumed by Jesus and also by His followers, James and John. It is a final comprehension of Jesus' overcommunicated message and a continuation of their shared vision.

Again in Luke 22:27, Jesus asks, "For who is greater, the one who is at the table or the one who serves? Is it not the one who is at the table? But I am among you as one who serves." In 1 John 3:16, Jesus encourages, "Let us not love with words...but with actions." There was such cohesion to the vision of Christ's ministry, and He was in the habit of repeating it because He knew His time on Earth was brief.

As a church, never shy away from overstating the vision. At Glad Tidings, our vision is "helping people become fully devoted followers of Jesus Christ," so we arrange everything else around that center. Our vision statement is printed in our weekly bulletin, decorates our pens, and is written on the street sign in front of the church so even if someone is driving by, they know what we are about. We aim to educate every person who walks through our church doors about our vision and want every person who serves to be aware of the vision. The worship team, the greeters, the cleaning crew, and children's ministry workers know that as they scrub, change diapers, sing, and converse, they are propelling forward the vision of helping people become fully devoted followers of Jesus Christ. It breathes life into those who volunteer in ministry when they are constantly reminded about why they serve.

2. Celebrating the Wins when People Live Out Vision

I have heard that "you can't drive forward by looking through the rearview mirror." I agree completely, but as we drive forward, I think there are necessary pit stops worthy for the stopping. These vital rest points revitalize the journey and inspire people. One of the pit stops that the church should remember is to stop and celebrate the wins of people living out vision.

There is a man at the church who we call "Commander Serve." Ken Cooper is the guy at the church who calls all the new visitors to follow up and ask how they are doing. He also assists new recruits in the SERVE process and helps people find their niche. But Ken wasn't always your typical church guy. He was redeemed from the dead-end lifestyle of a cocaine addict when he decided to serve Jesus. Once he realized how much time had been wasted living selfishly, he was motivated to help others as much as he could. So guess what Ken did? He donated one of his kidneys to a complete stranger. Is that hands-on service or what? He heard about a desperate need and responded. Thanks to Ken's willingness to serve, he literally saved a woman's life. I think that is a story worth celebrating—when a former drug addict wakes up one day and decides that he wants to serve the kingdom by loving in such a tangible way.

Someone else inspired Ken. Her name was Sarah. At the time, Sarah was working in the church office as the secretary. One day, she was given a very mundane task. To prepare for the weekend service, Sarah was asked to tape fifteen hundred mustard seeds individually to pieces of paper, which would be handed out to each person in the service as a visual illustration of Jesus' words. In Matthew 17:20, Jesus encourages, "If you have faith as small as a mustard seed, you can say to this mountain, 'Move from here to there,' and it will move." Again, in Matthew 13:31–32, He says, "The kingdom of heaven is like a mustard seed, which a man took and planted in his field. Though it is the smallest of all seeds, yet when it grows, it is the largest of garden plants and becomes a tree, so that the birds come and perch in its branches."

If you have ever held a mustard seed, they are so small that they normally slip into the wrinkles of your palm. When you look at a mustard seed, it does not evoke thoughts of potential or grandeur. Yet Jesus chose a mustard seed as His example. Isn't Jesus always embodying His message with the least likely models? We choose wealth, promotion, status, and fashion. But Jesus chooses women, children, servants, and mustard seeds. Jesus explains that it doesn't take much; the smallest efforts will yield great results if faith is involved.

Let's go back to Ken. When Ken walked into church that day, he was still new in his faith. He received the paper with the mustard seed taped on it. Holding the mustard seed in his hand during the service, he began to wonder about the kind of person who would spend his or her time performing such a monotonous assignment. And something clicked within him. He realized he wasn't the kind of person who would do something like that. But he wanted to be. Ken was then motivated to start serving in small, humble ways and began seeking out different veins of service. He volunteered at the church in the behind-the-scenes areas. He specifically asked for the jobs that no one wanted to do. Eventually, he even gave his own kidney.

Talk about the great harvest of a small mustard seed! Sarah served in a small way, and she inspired Ken who was later inspired to donate a vital organ to a total stranger. Now Ken inspires people on a regular basis to serve at the church. And I'm sure many of them have their own stories to tell.

Celebrate the wins. It is important to tell the stories of those in your church who are living out vision in real and exciting ways. Bring these stories to life by retelling them and watch them bear fruit by taking a pit stop and celebrating the wins.

3. Encouraging the Visionaries

Not everyone has to be a visionary, but everyone should have a vision. Within ministry there are several roles. There is the leadership level, which in our vernacular ought to be servant leadership. These are the visionaries—the ones who create the vision, tighten the vision, and remind others about the vision. Oftentimes, they are the pastors, ministry leaders, board members, and those at other levels of leadership. And then there are the volunteers. They are the people who hear the vision and carry it out. In the church both are equally important, but it is important to be able to recognize the visionaries and encourage them to lead.

Oftentimes, you can find the visionaries by seeking out the people who have the most passion. I have never met someone who is a visionary who is also dull. Vision always coincides with passion. Passion makes the ordinary a visionary. Passion in a person becomes them, and they become like their passion. I love the way a passionate person beams when they talk about what excites them. I love to see a person who is stirred up by life.

Have you ever talked to someone who is practically jumping out of their skin because they are invigorated by a passion? I've talked to missionaries who speak and raise funds because they are determined to take the gospel message to a particular region of the world. I've sat in antisex trafficking meetings where police officers and government workers share their determination to put an end to the sex slave industry in US cities. I've read books by men like Shane Claiborne and Dick Brogden, "ordinary radicals" whose passion for Jesus jumps off the pages of their books. When people birth a vision, it always stems from a passion.

During a part-time job at a local bookstore, I worked with a girl named Rebecca, who hated her job. It was almost commendable how she always managed to find something to complain about. After a couple weeks of working together, someone mentioned her husband, and I saw a transformation take place in her. Her entire demeanor reversed from misery to delight. Her eyes began to sparkle. She smiled. It was revolutionary. From that day on, every time she was irritable, I would mention her husband and watch the renovation occur. The change occurred because I discovered what Rebecca was passionate about. Passion has the ability to transform.

It is not ironic then that the crucifixion of Christ is referred to as the Passion. In a broad sense, passion has the ability to change a person, but Christ's passion had the ability to change the world. His passion was all-encompassing and came to completion through His final act of service to us—death on a cross. John Maxwell said, "A great leader's courage to fulfill his vision comes from passion, not position."[14] If Jesus had been concerned about His position, He would never have lowered Himself to the stance of a servant. Instead, Jesus was steadfast in His passion.

We don't all need to be the visionaries, but it is essential that every church has visionaries. As long as churches are generating vision, the volunteers will naturally exude the momentum of it. Continue or start to raise up leaders within your church. Keep an eye out for the passionate ones because even if they are not leader material at the moment, they could be future visionaries in the making.

4. Setting Strategic Goals

The last way that a church shares the same vision is by setting strategic goals. The whimsical side of me wants to title this section "The Dream Generator." Here comes the portion of vision that establishes

14   John C. Maxwell, *The 21 Indispensable Qualities of a Leader: Becoming the Person That People Will Want to Follow* (Nashville, TN: T. Nelson, 1999).

benchmarks. It dreams God-sized dreams. It sets a finish line. The reason why strategic goals are important for a church is because ministry can become quite daunting. For example, our vision at Glad Tidings is "helping people become fully devoted followers of Jesus Christ," and although it is an excellent vision, it is extremely open-ended. It seems to have no clear start or finish, nor does it explain any plausible means of accomplishment. How are we supposed to help people learn about Jesus? Who is our target people group? Once established into the faith, how does the church plan to disciple people? Questions like these lead us to strategic goals to help carry out the vision.

Strategic goals have different characteristics from vision. Strategic goals usually have a deadline as opposed to vision, which is usually timeless. Strategic goals are normally defined by benchmarks, such as numbers and statistics. Also, strategic goals have more flexibility than vision. Vision should be refined, and goals should be defined. Lastly, strategic goals should fit into the vision, not the other way around.

At GT, our strategic goals are set within a five-year plan. In other words, they offer us a chance to dream about how the church could impact the community within the next five years. Mark Batterson writes about steering a passion by setting a goal.

A goal is a passion with a deadline. A goal is a way of breaking a dream down into steps and stages. Nehemiah gives himself a deadline. Nehemiah 2:6 says, "I set a time" ...I think ideas have an expiration date or shelf life. If you don't act on them, they get stale and eventually moldy until the dream rots. That is the

best description I can give of a God-given dream, passion, or goal that isn't acted upon. What would have nourished us begins to poisons us. The blessing becomes a curse.

That is precisely what Proverbs 29:18 says, "Where there is no vision, the people perish." The word perish refers to fruit that is past its ripeness and beginning to rot. If you don't have a God-sized goal you're going after, it begins to eat you up inside. I know that not everyone is Nehemiah. Not everybody is called to rebuild the wall of Jerusalem. But all of us need spiritual and relational and occupational goals ...[15]

As Batterson says, we create a five-year plan because deadlines keep us focused. Once we establish our goals, we put them into print and commit to them wholeheartedly. Some of our goals are ideas for special services, community events, and outreach opportunities. Some goals involve a targeted number of baptisms, salvations, and new visitors. Pastor Bryan articulates that we set numerical goals, not because numbers matter but because people matter. The numbers are a way for us to stay attentive to the people we reach, and it also helps us to gauge the number of unreached people in Berks County.

Within the last decade, we have seen results from our strategic goals like a new sanctuary, an addition to our building, and an online church. These goals create energy and stimulate motivation for service. Strategic goals are crucial to the church and ministry, but God-sized dreams can also exist within our personal life.

When was the last time you remember having a dream that was much bigger than you? A huge indicator of a God-dream is that its purposes are grander than your own fulfillment or enjoyment. Are you dreaming for the sake of your own happiness or for the sake of

15   Mark Batterson, *"The Game of Life: Setting God-Sized Goals,"* www. markbatterson.com (web log), July 9, 2005, http://www.markbatterson.com.

glorifying God? Do you dream about the big ways that you can love and serve people? Or do you dream about your own adventures, romance, and success? Again, Jesus would direct us toward a heart for serving.

Although failures can flip our vision sideways and set our dreams backward, Jesus redefines the terms of each. His vision and dreams are all about becoming less, giving more, and finding peace in the have-nots. His goals are completely flipped upside down. They change us from the innermost part. John Mark Comer quoted, "Humility is not thinking less of yourself. It is thinking nothing of yourself."[16] God is calling each one of us to be humble dream generators. Dream big for the sake of the kingdom.

Serve as Life Vision

One afternoon, I sat at our kitchen table, brooding over a cup of coffee, lacking the words to write. I had been studying the message of serve in the Gospels, and I had hit a wall. I was mentally exhausted because I felt that Jesus was asking so much from us, and I was not sure I was up for it. My dad walked in, and I started venting.

"I don't understand it," I said, spilling out my doubts and frustrations. "All the things in the world I can try to make sense of—art, music, culture, emotion—but I am disturbed by Jesus' message of service. It asks so much of us." I looked at him, feeling very small and desperate for understanding. "Have you ever wondered if it's worth it? I know you're a pastor, but honestly, have you ever questioned it? Is a life of service worth all of the effort it requires of us?"

He thought about it for a few moments. Then he looked at me and said, "Courtney, when I'm gone, you will hopefully remember me for many honorable things, many good things. But your mom—you'll remember her for the way that she served. You will remember the way

---

16   John Mark Comer, "Philippians: A Colony of Heaven," *Solid Rock Church* (audio blog), section goes here, accessed July 23, 2013, http://www.ajesuschurch.org/philippians-series/?sermon_id=918.

that she lived for others. I don't think a person could leave the world with anything greater."

Chapter Summary

» Jesus' vision is the unifying force that binds together each eclectic movement of believers.

» If the entire body of Christ shared the same vision and acted on it, we would be an unstoppable force!

» The vision of a church must be consistently verbalized in order for it to be effective.

» One of the pit stops that a church should remember is to stop and celebrate the wins of people living out the vision.

» Humble service inspires grand results.

» Serving sets in motion a chain reaction that prompts ripples of service by others.

» Vision coincides with passion.

» Passion has the ability to transform.

» A goal is a passion with a deadline.

» Goals create energy and stimulate motivation for service.

Questions

» Do you know what Christ's vision is for the church?

» Do you know the specific vision statement of your church?

» How have you engaged in the vision of your church?

» Do you have a personal life vision? If so, what is it?

» What are you most passionate about? What creates natural excitement and passion for you?

» When considering your life vision and passion, what goals can you set for yourself to work toward accomplishing?

2 embrace excellence

O ccasionally, I write with a knit hat hugging my messy morning tresses. When I do so, I imagine that I am Jo from Little Women, hidden upstairs in my attic, feverishly writing a masterpiece. In our small suburb of Pennsylvania, our home is beginning to resemble

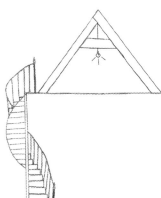

Christmas with the garland's inaugural display and the eggnog's introduction onto our refrigerator shelves. These small indicators edge my thoughts toward Alcott's novel. I always admired the spirited protagonist for her tenacity. There was a lot of fight in her; her passion was so alive. When she wrote, she crafted tales of adventure and romance with a zealous devotion. Her dedication to her work as a writer was tangible. And she always seemed to be moved by the same underlying force: Greatness. She wanted to become a great writer.

As I type away, the pitter-patter of the keys weaving words into sentences, I wrestle with greatness. I could fill page after page with empty sentences, sentences that lack meaning and have no felt significance to either you or me. But in that case, why make any feeble attempt? And yet greatness is a treacherous thought. How does one achieve it? How do we reach it? The stakes seem so high. And yet it is what we all long for.

Aspiring toward greatness is that small thing inside each one of us that hopes. It is the hope that our lives will amount to something. Or perhaps it is the opposite—the battle against the fear that we have lived inconsequentially. And these thoughts hang over the edges of my mind as I work, hoping the words situating themselves onto these pages will either be a product of greatness or an instigator of it.

You are either an individual reading this book about serving or a church developing a culture of serving. In either case, I hope you aspire toward greatness, but do not define it in terms of commercial success as we so often do. Do not define it by the skill level of your task or the numerical count of your church attendance. View the idea of greatness as both large and small tasks executed with excellence.

Inefficiency Toward Greatness

There are many ways to move efficiently toward greatness. But I am going to bestow you with a new venture: Aim to be inefficient in your greatness. Seriously. As Nelson Searcy phrased it, I encourage you to descend toward greatness.[1]

1   Nelson Searcy and Jennifer Dykes. Henson, The Greatness Principle: Finding Significance and Joy by Serving Others (Grand Rapids, MI: Baker Books, 2012).

We are living in a unique age in American history when even professional success or greatness is becoming less corporate, less efficient. Extra effort seems to be gaining the extra attention. It's the evolution of what is being referred to as the "Artisan Economy," where artisans are rising up and offering more specialized products and buyers are thankful for it. There is a growing desire for organic, fairtrade, or specialized goods. A greater attention to detail in the art form is replacing what used to be the machine of production. Although mass production is more cost-friendly, it is beginning to lose its kitschy appeal and is slightly less tantalizing. It is the difference between a chain restaurant and a privately owned one. It's the difference between "Made in China" and "Made in Our Backyard." Professor Charles Heying from Portland State University said,

No matter what sort of economic justifications they offered, people began to recognize these corporations treated people and places as if they were entirely replaceable parts in their calculus of efficiency. Likewise, the commodities these de-localized corporations produce have become so homogenous, tasteless, and soulless, they opened a space for artisans who could produce things that were interesting, tasteful, distinct, and that made connections between the real people who made things and the real people who bought them.[2]

A similar pattern seems to be emerging within the church. Many churches are following the patterns of mega-churches and are moving away from specialization toward generalization. Because several churches are so dynamic in how they do church, other churches default to replication. Whatever appears dynamic in the moment, we try to copy. But the danger with replicating a standard church mold is that we lose specialization. We lose this artisan mentality and the breeding of originality.

Each church has a basic desire to aspire toward greatness like

---

2   Maggie Shafer, "The Artisan Economy," Relevant Magazine: Issue 59, September/October 2012.

any other organization. But what does greatness look like within the church? Beside the nonnegotiables like doctrine and the ordinances, what does a church look like in its endeavors to be both relevant and truthful? I think that many pastors, church leaders, and volunteers have asked themselves this same question. Unfortunately, the easiest answer is found in replication. That is why smaller churches look to larger, more "successful" churches and duplicate what they see. Doing church this way avoids culturally outdated faux pas, but it also avoids greatness. What gets lost is a direct correlation between a church and its specific region. Rick Warren, pastor of Saddleback Church, would wear Hawaiian shirts when he preached. This worked in Southern California where his church is located. But it wouldn't work in Philly. Bill Hybels from Willow Creek leads with a corporate philosophy of ministry, but this works in Chicago, which is in the shadow of Fortune 500 companies. It wouldn't work in rural Pennsylvania. Churches try to copy what they see instead of becoming attuned to the culture within their region. Tragically, they then lose this beautiful sense of authenticity. It trickles from top leadership to key volunteers to the people who fill its seats, for everything becomes a replica, a chain church, and creative energies comes to a halt.

I challenge you, both individually and as a church community, to return to Jesus' model of greatness. Not Andy Stanley's, Mark Driscoll's, or Bill Hybel's, although we can find inspiration and gain insight from each of them. I've found that the red letters in the pages of Scripture are always the best place to start. And, I might also add, the best place to end.

When the disciples are walking to Capernaum, they are caught mid-conversation discussing who among them is the greatest. Imagine walking back from a ministry event with Jesus, and you are off in a side conversation, discussing which one of your posse is the greatest. It sounds audacious. It also sounds very human. Jesus later responds to them with this: "If anyone wants to be first, he must be the very last, and the servant of all" (Mark 9:35). Basically, Jesus flips their tables of arrogance upside down. He sets the record straight, once and for all, that His measurement for greatness is far removed from their scales.

Being great by Jesus' standards is appallingly inefficient. The most outrageous act of greatness and service was hanging on a cross-shaped tree. For many who had their hopes stored in a Messiah, this must have seemed incredibly inefficient. But Jesus' road toward greatness is one that is paved by the inefficient marks of sacrifice, surrender, and service.

From this vantage point, the only way up is down. Striving toward greatness is a task, and it is not for the faint of heart. But as Jesus made clear, it starts with service—excellent service. Not just service that was mediocre or somewhere in the middle. Jesus does not ask you to let a few people ahead of you in line. He demands that you get to the very back of the line and then ask if anyone else wants to get in front of you. You want to descend toward greatness? Then sign up for excellence in your service.

Churches, volunteers, and leaders, be gentle toward yourselves and your ministries. Greatness looks so different from Jesus' eyes than from the eyes of onlookers. But this is good news. When you realize that greatness looks different from what you thought, it opens up this vast freedom to create, dream, work collectively within our church bodies, and be authentic exposés of Christ.

Extravagant, Over-the-Top Service

We can all recall specific restaurants, hotels, or dinner parties that have impressed us due to the caliber of service. We remember the over-the-top menu or the lush spatial adornments. Extravagant circumstances launch us into moments of wonder. These experiences are memorable because excellent service leaves an imprint upon us. Although we are creatures of monotony, we are drawn toward excellence. For our morning coffee, we prefer the coffee shop where we are greeted by name and our latte is created to perfection. Our choice of salon or barbershop is dictated by the credibility of our stylist and his or her ability to cut and color with a slim percentage of error. Once we find a stylist we trust, we return as their client since he or she has earned our approval through excellent service tailored to our unique needs. When we receive over-the-top service, we recognize the value in it. Most of us have the mentality that the more we pay, the better quality we receive. And it is a price we are willing to pay, the purchase of excellence. But what if excellence didn't have to come at a cost?

Picture yourself pulling up to a car wash. Five workers come out and scrub, vacuum, and shine your car until it glistens under the bright sun. Your car looks as good as the day you bought it. Proud of their work, you walk inside to pay, and they respond, "Today it's on the house!" You would be taken aback. The car wash exemplified service that emanated excellence and reflected highly upon the company. But it was next-level service to add this element of kindness, completely unearned and unexpected. We are not familiar with receiving extreme measures of excellence without paying a high price. Not only would this make us feel special but maybe even uncomfortable, as if we are now indebted to someone.

Although occurrences like this are rare, what if every community had one specific place that was known for this kind of service? What if this place had a reputation for continual, over-the-top service flowing outwardly in exchange for nothing? That place would easily become admired and respected within the community, and the community would regularly seek its services.

Now what if this place was the church?

The saddest part of this whimsical idea is that it should be the church. As Christ-followers, we have willingly signed up for a life of extravagant, over-the-top service. So where have we gone wrong? Why does the church lack this reputation? We seek out excellence in all other systems but then neglect the church. In replacement, the church is oftentimes labeled as greedy, judgmental, and closed-minded. However, the church model demonstrated by Jesus classifies itself as fully committed to service with attention to people, details, and lavish generosity. It is time that the church shifts its focus from mediocre inwardness to philanthropic excellence.

Q: Think of a time when you received excellent, extravagant service. What qualities made it stand out?

Q: When have you lavished someone else with this kind of service without expecting anything in return? How did it feel?

Q: How can the church do a better job within your community of serving extravagantly?

Q: Choose an area in your own life where you will commit to exacting more detail and effort for the sake of excellence in your service.

Compliments of the Chef

My first waitress job is a sore memory. Mentally, I evaluated the list of qualifications to become a waitress and thought, I got this. I applied, interviewed, and was hired. My first day on the job was on Valentine's Day weekend. The translation for Valentine's Day in the restaurant world is "pure insanity." With the holiday's arrival, the restaurant could not afford the

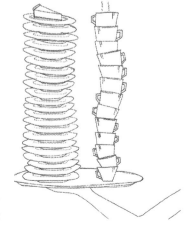

time to train me, so I was unleashed into the chaos like a lamb to a pack of hungry wolves (which we will get to shortly). The restaurant was bustling with activity. Trays, drinks, and bussers whirled around me. Not even the national day of love could distract the couples seated at my tables from my slow onslaught of panic. New tables were being seated faster than I could say, "Help! I'm drowning here!"

The only night equally as demoralizing was a week later when an entire minor league hockey team was seated in my section. As Murphy and his law ensure, everything that could go awry, did. I botched food orders, interwove check items, and even incorrectly charged credit cards. After being employed at the restaurant for three months, I surprisingly quit before I was fired. But I assure you that my abilities as a waitress were never a picture of excellence.

Nevertheless, I learned a valuable lesson. Without cognitively thinking about it at the time, I was learning how to serve more than food. I was learning how to serve people. Each day, when I knotted on my apron, I was enlisting myself into service for the next five to eight hours; I was dressing myself to serve. Although it was a paid service, my job by nature required me to anticipate others needs before my own. I was earning a wage by becoming available to people who I had no level of relationship with, neither knowing nor being known. I was serving complete strangers because I was representing my employer, the restaurant. Whether service is done poorly or with excellence, it is always a reflection of the larger embodiment. It is the branding of the company. The service can either accent the experience with delight or taint it with distaste.

Since my restaurant stint, I have become acutely aware of the attending service at restaurants. On a recent vacation to the Carolinas, we ate dinner at a fine restaurant. Between the appetizer and entrée, the waiter surprised us with a round of gourmet crab cakes. He introduced it as a "compliment of the chef." It was a subtle reminder that the rich surroundings, chandeliers, thick mahogany wood, and pristine table settings were all accents of the centerpiece—the chef's work. The chef, hidden in the kitchen, was the originator of the sustenance. The excellent service was a reflection of the master chef. As Christ-followers we are called to be servants—servers. We are called to reflect the master chef and be the deliverers of sustenance. So, how are we doing Church? Is the church a place that is reflecting the excellence of our Master? Are we leaving the people who walk in and out of our doors every week with novelty or a sour distaste for the gospel message? Are we as Christ-followers striving for excellence in our service, being attentive to the needs of people, and dishing out hearty helpings of the attributes of Jesus? Sometimes perhaps, but overall, I fear we are settling for mediocrity, reflecting subpar semblances of our Master. As Erwin McManus, lead pastor of Mosaic Church in Los Angeles, says, "At our worst, we are creatives informed by darkness rather than light. At our best, we create such beauty that it brings glory to God and hope to the world."[3]

Reflect God's Greatness

Generally, the ins-and-outs of our daily lives lack the extraordinary. Picking up the kids from baseball practice, sitting in traffic, making dinner, doing income taxes—they are the routines that make up the fabric of our lives. Occasionally, an awe-inspiring glimpse of the extraordinary occurs, but the feelings of fireworks and Christmas morning is not the norm, which is okay. "Normal" is healthy. It is the table on which we eat, the enduring furniture of our lives nourishing us with a pace and a rhythm. However, as Christians, we have been called to transcendence, sought out to live in the light of a transcendent Being, which means extending beyond the ordinary.

Normality is a reality of our lives, but it is not a truth about God's character. The Bible clearly depicts God as extravagant. Isaiah

---

3   Maggie Shafer, "The Artisan Economy," *Relevant Magazine*: Issue 59, September/October 2012.

encourages, "Lift your eyes and look to the heavens. Who created all these? He who brings out the starry hosts one by one and calls them each by name. Because of His great power and mighty strength, not one of them is missing" (Isaiah 40:26). Another reverberates His declaration, "I Am the LORD; that is my name! I will not give my glory to another or my praise to idols" (Isaiah 42:8). God titles Himself "I Am," declaring His sovereignty over all things. In the New Testament, God reveals Himself in a different form of creation, but equally as extravagant, through His Son, Jesus. Jesus reveals a different facet of God's extravagance through His miracles and sinless nature. When Jesus came to Earth, "The Artist became oil on his own palette. The Potter melted into the mud on His own wheel."[4] Through Jesus' life and the creation of the earth, God's transcendence is displayed. How easily we forget that God's goodness in our lives is anything but normal or ordinary. It is excellent and extravagant.

As Christians, we must renew our energies for revealing the awe-inspiring attributes of God. If we did so, it would be utterly flabbergasting and awe-inspiring. In Psalm 34:8, David beckons us to "Taste and see that the Lord is good." Solomon expresses how God "has taken me to the banquet hall, and His banner over me is love" (Song of Solomon 2:4). Friends, when are we going to begin to treat Christianity like it is something to be excited about? When are we going to see the church like it is worthy of our attention, availability, and efforts? Have we ourselves tasted and seen that the Lord is good? Is His excellence a reality in our own lives and outwardly expressed through the work of our hands?

God told His chosen people, "You are my servant, Israel, in whom I will display my splendor" (Isaiah 49:3). If restaurants are able to compliment the reputation of their chefs through their service, how much more is the church capable of doing likewise? Noma, voted the

---

4   Max Lucado, God's Story, Your Story: When His Becomes Yours (Grand Rapids, MI: Zondervan, 2011).

best restaurant in the world in 2012, was attributed as "a restaurant of extraordinary pedigree, where passion and honesty is reflected."[5] Holding third place, the restaurant Mugaritz's review states, "It is a place where diners go to have their preconceptions of food smashed to pieces. Its dishes are designed to tell a story, evoke an emotion, and bring some magic to the dining experience." [6]

Can you imagine if the church received reviews like this for Christ's sake? What if people walked out of the church with their negative preconceptions about God smashed to pieces? Whether people admire or despise the church, let us not give them any reason to have distaste toward us. I would love to hear "Passion and honesty were reflected there" leave the lips of those walking out the church doors on Sunday mornings. Within its interior, allow the church to tell a story, evoke an emotion, and spur forth something unearthly.

An Opening Line to Remember

Do you fall for the stunning first lines of a book? Those lines that project excellence from the start. Look at the Bible. "In the beginning, God created ..." (Genesis 1:1). The first five words already reveal characteristics about our main character! He clearly existed from the beginning. He was first. And He was already creating. His hand was already fabricating, working, orchestrating, molding, and forming. This artisan was creatively at work from the moment of His introduction. It introduces a God I want to read more about.

Many famous speeches through the ages have gained their repute from line one. Martin Luther King Jr.'s opener, "I have a dream," or Abraham Lincoln's "Four score and seven years ago." These one-liners

---

5   Stefan Chomka, "Noma," EDE ONLINE, section goes here, accessed July 22, 2013, http://www.eat-drink-etc.com/articles/noma.

6   "The World's 50 Best Restaurants 2013," The World's 50 Best, Mugaritz, accessed July 22, 2013, http://www.theworlds50best.com/awards/chefs-choice/?chocaid=397.

greet us as the concise passageways into richly developed messages of provocative rhetoric. And these lines begin stories of greatness.

In Luke 10, Jesus begins our stories with a memorable first line. He gathers the volunteers together like a pre-event rally, and His initial words to them are a doozy. I imagine chatter and the excitement of the volunteers as they are mingling amongst themselves, and then Jesus stands up to speak. He begins with, "Go! I am sending you out like lambs among wolves!" (Luke 10:3)

No one wants to hear those words during the opening of a pep talk. Jesus' words consistently catch me off guard. If you were embarking on a trip, your spouse, parent, or friend might warn you of some potential dangers, but essentially, they would send you off with a cheery bon voyage. One of the top ten things they probably would not say is "You will be like a lamb among wolves!" Jesus is clearly priming these volunteers for a conversation of intensity without intonations of fluff and frills. Jesus had them from hello.

Leave the Bags. Bring on the Wolves.

The portrayal of a lamb among wolves is a depiction that cannot be easily misinterpreted. Lambs are docile, passive creatures, cloaked in

white, representing cleanliness or innocence. In contrast, the wolves represent that which is ferocious, menacing, and violent. Therefore, the imagery of a lamb among a pack of wolves leans more toward a tragedy than a comedy. Jesus is warning them from the start that serving is not an easy task. He places an incredibly heavy statement as the stepping block into service.

If the pastor or head recruiter at your church told you that working in the kid's ministry would be similar to being thrown into a pack of wolves, would you be energized and eager to join the team? Probably not. In fact, you might opt for a different department. Although Jesus' first sentence is daunting, we can appreciate the honesty. We also see the weight of the job that is being entrusted. Although these poor volunteers may have been intimidated like young soldiers going off to battle, at least they were aware of the significance and magnitude of the call. One commentary suggests that Jesus was trying to communicate that "He who is called to preach the Gospel is called to embrace a state of constant labor and frequent suffering."[7]

After Jesus breaks the ice, He continues to lead them down a path of further discomfort with "Do not take a purse or bag or sandals; and do not greet anyone on the road." [8] Aside from the unsettling first statement, the second is equally as dubious in nature. Do not pack belongings, and do not engage in conversation. Check.

Although this message seems peculiar, there is a distinct purpose for it. By instructing them not to bring anything with them, He is slowly stripping them of all vices. He wants them to distribute their faith differently. Jesus sends the volunteers out in pairs (Luke 10:1) because He knows that where material items would encumber their journey, a friend would bolster it.

With the direction to avoid greeting passersby, He is trying to eliminate distractions. In the first century, a greeting was not a mere hello as we would assume. It was a time-consuming, tedious process laden in rituals. Stopping for the appropriate greeting each time they walked by another person would prolong their journey, causing delay and loss of focus. Of course, Jesus was not encouraging His followers to be rude to others; He was trying to prevent the ambush of sideways

---

7   Adam Clarke, The New Testament of Our Lord and Saviour Jesus Christ; the Text...(New York: Methodist Book Concern, [..]).

8   Luke 10:4

energy. His whole ministry was defined by the run-in's He had with individuals along the journey, but for this specific time, He urged them to stay on task.

Jesus then continues to instruct the seventy-two disciples in what appears to be a "coaching moment" where He talks to them in an extremely structured, specific, and ordered manner. He gives them multiple "if-then" scenarios like "If a man of peace is there," then "your peace will rest on them" (Luke 10: 6) or "When you enter a town and are welcomed, eat what is set before you" and continues in this manner of speaking.

The verbal initiative here in Luke is core to understanding the proper way to behave as a servant of Christ. He packs it with specific scenarios and details. It encourages a regimented course of action, involving an acute attention to detail. And it communicates to church volunteers, like you and me, that service requires our devotion and intentionality. This biblical pep rally is cheering on focus and steadfastness for the coming tasks. But the best part is when Jesus ends with "All things have been committed to me by my Father. No one knows who the Father is except the Son and those to whom the Son chooses to reveal him" (Luke 10:22). This verse is our foundation and target. Essentially all of our striving for excellence is meaningless without pointing back to Jesus. At Starbucks, they pour great effort into their excellence, and it has proved to be a successful business model. However, for us as Christ-followers, it is more than just coffee and blueberry scones. Starbucks is creating an atmosphere and connection; for us, it is far more than that, and we cannot fail in our mission.

We can be thankful that the Son chooses to reveal the Father to His servants. We are His choice. After the seventy-two returned from their travels with joy, Jesus turns to them and says, "Blessed are the eyes that see what you see. For I tell you that many prophets and kings wanted to see what you see but did not see it and to hear what you hear but did not hear it" (Luke 10:23). So although Jesus is calling us to become lambs among wolves and leave all our baggage behind us, He promises that we will be blessed through our service.

Q: If you were one of the seventy-two volunteers, what would be the most intimidating part of Jesus' instructions?

Q: When you have the impulse to serve, what is normally your central hesitation?

Instructions to SERVE

Instructions are important, and I've learned that it is usually best to follow them. If you are stubborn like me, you probably prefer your own way, but this always takes longer. It is best to follow instructions. Have you ever answered one of those trick quizzes that tests your instruction-reading skills? You are meant to read all of the directions first. If you skip step one, you take the entire test only to discover at the end that you should have read step one: Disregard the rest of the test. Ignorance is not always bliss. The type A's heartily agree while the headstrong ones mumble their private disapproval. Rules and established order are a necessary part of life. Serving within the church should not be an exception, but oftentimes, it is treated like it is. In the corporate world, pace and order is expected. Most companies have a dress code, a punch card or salaried amount of hours, and a manual packed with rules to which each employee must comply. Yet in the church, everyone desires more leniencies, which hurts our degrees of excellence.

There are two mind-sets I have heard within the church. Here is the first: the program-led.

As Sunday approaches, the church staff prepares for the upcoming service. The worship team will play two upbeat songs and then two slow songs, which preferably coincide with the day's sermon topic.

The topic has been decided upon months in advance so that graphics, themes, and series can be developed. The pastor finalizes his message early so that the message notes can be printed for distribution. When it comes to announcements, the approaching events are written into a script for the communicator. The media team creates a short video to artistically display the message, which was filmed a month prior. And as all of the elements emerge, they are threaded together in a cohesive manner—the worship set, the announcements, the video, and the message. There are time restraints assigned to each. Five minutes for announcements. Twenty minutes for worship. Five minutes for video. Forty minutes for sermon. If all goes as planned, everyone should be out just in time for the second service. They are structured, organized and committed to giving their best. This is an example of a church that uses their efforts, careful planning, and thematic input to create an ordered, time-conscious service.

The second mind-set is the supposed opposite: the spirit-led.

There are several people who attend the church explained above. After service, they leave in want. They remember the days when there was only one service. Sometimes the pastor would preach for over an hour, and no one cared that it ran late because the spirit was moving. They remember a time when the pastor preached what God laid on his heart earlier that morning. Oh, how God spoke directly to them that morning! And why did the worship team stop playing after the fourth song? The Lord was clearly moving!

Where is room for the Holy Spirit amid careful planning? Do we think that we can do church on our own? Is the spontaneity of God's powerful presence being seized by the church's structured service agendas? "We just wish that the services were more spirit-led and less program-led," people say.

These are the very opposing mind-sets of the church. You can see the clear clash, causing division within the church. In the program-led model, there is a distinct mirroring of excellence, yet it offends the value system of the spirit-led. So the big question is, Which is correct? And it is a dangerous question, which I approach with caution. I have visited both types of churches and left dissatisfied by both extremes. From the program-led, I have felt stifled by the structure and regiment of the services. From the spirit-led, I have felt embarrassed by the lack of preparation and order. So I ask, Which represents the kind of church Jesus would have orchestrated?

We search Luke 10 for an answer. In it, we find that Jesus was extremely deliberate about the structure of His ministry. He was specific about the order, and He asked volunteers to follow instructions. Therefore, would Jesus side with programs? Not necessarily. In His instructions, He asks that they pay attention to the spiritual thermostat. He wants the volunteers to tune in to their audience and choose their actions based on these observations. He asks them to perform miracles and healings in His name, only if the town is open to it (Luke 10:9). What we see is a passage laden with detailed instructions rooted out of an acute sensitivity to the Spirit. This is not an easy answer since it requires a search for balance. And as a church, we will not always get it right. But at least we have a target to aim toward.

Let's be real. "Spirit-led" should never be our excuse for laziness. Jesus never sought to recruit idle servants. If a pastor wants to forgo his sermon notes based on God's prompting, he should do so. Yet God's spirit does not always manifest itself through spontaneity. Sometimes God's spirit works through our labors. Our sweat and tears are often the precursors to God's fruitfulness. The church is not the place to wing it under the name of divine intervention. When we are told that the harvest is plentiful and the workers are few, He is clearly telling us that He needs workers, emphasis on the "work." Prayer is a part of the work, but so is hands-on action. As Christ-followers, let us create a reputation for being hard workers, both within and outside of the church walls. Let us be a people who companies are eager to hire, regardless of faith, because those who carry Jesus' name are people famous for their hard work, integrity, and degree of excellence. If you are on the worship team, schedule practices, create a song order, and make the most beautiful music you are capable of. If you are on the facilities and grounds team, cut the grass, shovel the sidewalk, and maintain an immaculate landscape. The appearance of the building and grounds is the first impression most people will have of the church before a hello, a handshake, or the pastor's message. Practice, preparation, and hard work are the vital signs of a commitment to excellence.

Our Church's Top Ten Ways to Serve with Excellence

1. Contact your leader if you are unable to be there
2. Check in when you arrive
3. Wear your nametag
4. Come early, stay late
5. Attend pre-service huddle or prayer time with your team
6. Connect with leader for specific instructions
7. Come prepared for your specific ministry
8. Be present in body, mind, and spirit
9. Stay healthy—Continue to grow spiritually
10. Connect—Be relational with your team

These simple steps communicate to each volunteer what is expected of them as they serve. Volunteers, do not underestimate your influence. Within the first seven minutes, new visitors decide if they will come back to the church, which is oftentimes before they even sit in the worship center. Therefore, the parking lot, the signage, the greeters and even the person sitting in the same row, all have a profound impact on whether or not a new guest will return a second time. Embrace excellence, because the small ways you serve can make big impressions.

Follow-Through

Everyone has at least one job that they hated. For my sister and me, it was the summer of strawberry picking. It sounded like a dream. As the sun peeked over the rolling fields, lush strawberry fields blossoming with fruit, we would make our way to the farm. Our days would be spent roving through the strawberry-speckled rows in the summer warmth, picking at our leisure and eating our heart's content of plump berries.

Best of all, we were doing it with friends, and anything is the most fun with friends, especially in junior high. I have always been an idealist. You know those people who fabricate unrealistic scenarios in their minds, always headed down the road of inevitable  disappointment? Nice to meet you.

The first day we woke up before the sun's arrival and were dropped off at the farm. Still yawning but with eyes glowing, we crowded into the back of a pickup truck with others looking much less enthusiastic. We were dropped off in the center of the field with our bright blue cartons. The berry picking commenced. It was one of the least romantic experiences of my life. The berries were infested with bugs and defects, and with my articulate eye for perfection, I discarded berry after berry. By day's end, I had hardly filled enough cartons to make half of minimum wage. In addition, I was tired and sweaty. And I was already sick of eating strawberries. The next day, only half of our friends came back, and by the third day, all had resigned, bar my sister and me. Calling a meeting to order, we met with our parents the next evening and announced that we were finished. Our strawberry picking days were in the past. We gave it our best but really didn't see a future in it.

To our surprise, our request was denied. My father was adamant. His philosophy was that we made a commitment, and we were going to stick to it. We elected our summer job and were going to fulfill our commitment through the remainder of strawberry-picking season. And so we did.

You know, I never learned to like strawberry picking, but I did learn something else that summer that turned out to be much more important. I learned what it looked like to follow through with a task, regardless of the task. I also learned about the value of dedication. I acquired a mind-set that was recycled throughout many situations in my life. Like when I enrolled in gymnastics class, became a college resident assistant, and even as an adult when I worked as a receptionist, follow-through was a humbling skill that built stamina. It taught me what uncompromising investment looked like, not based on preference but rather on commitment.

True excellence necessitates follow-through. You can have glimpses of excellence without it; there is always the possibility of one-hit wonders in ministry. As a graphic designer, I could create an out-of-the-park design for a single brochure in the church and then call it quits, but the kind of excellence that Jesus calls us to requires longevity. He wants us to set up camp. As in most things Jesus asks us to do, true excellence requires an investment. It is easy to strive for excellence once or twice, but to strive for excellence on a regular basis with a constant relinquishment of personal preference is a different caliber of service. Excellence done with follow-through is not "when I feel like it" service. Nor is it "good enough" service. It is executed with a commitment to top-notch service for the long haul, and this kind of service honors God.

But for volunteers, serving is often their free time! It's their elected hobby, their other hours outside of the nine-to-five workday. So it is very easy for volunteers to justify inconsistencies in their level of commitment. I know because I'm guilty of it! On some days, service will feel like a dream job, and other days, it will feel like strawberry picking on a sweltering summer day. But follow-through is necessary on both occasions. Church ministries rely heavily on the involvement of volunteers, so a ministry could not function if the volunteers were not dependable. The church would suffer greatly from halfhearted volunteers who only served when they felt like it. This would be detrimental to the church and also disobedient to Jesus' call to service. If service truly means an abandonment of self, it means that we must see our commitments to fulfillment.

When the church has committed volunteers, the church has better volunteers. When I think of excellent service, I think of Lucille who works in the church office week after week. She is about eighty years old, loves Jesus, and has the best stories. If we need papers shredded, cut, folded, or counted, she is the woman for the job. Like clockwork, Lucille calls the office every Tuesday with "Do ya need me?" And each week, she comes in and does her job. The amazing part is I think Lucille needs us as much as we need her. Through her diligence, she has become a necessity to the office, making her time and assistance a genuine asset to the staff. Additionally, we have built a community in which Lucille is an essential part. We have become quite necessary to each other, and this is the beauty of service. It integrates people on a much deeper level, ingratiating each other together through our service while also building our skills, developing our commitment levels, and releasing our stubborn right to selfishness.

Overall, volunteers function better in a consistent area of ministry with the same people having the same passion for ministry. It's the best way to do life together. We grow our talents. We develop a greater sense of ownership in our ministry areas. It is exciting to feel like we are a part of something, and when we are invested, we naturally thrive. At Willow Creek, the director of programming writes,

> "The value of excellence first permeates the hearts of individuals ...People joyfully show up expecting to serve with their sleeves rolled up, their minds fully engaged, and their radars on high alert to discern potential improvements. We've learned that devotion to excellence really does inspire our visitors. They come to church for the first time expecting it to be second-rate and thrown together. When they experience the opposite, they are both surprised and motivated to investigate the faith behind the quality."[9]

Follow-through and devotion is a characteristic that is clearly depicted in Luke 10 when Jesus instructs them not to move from house to house (Luke 10:7) when they find a place they are welcomed. Jesus wants them to receive nourishment from one solitary place and in turn heal their sick and share the news of the gospel. I hear Jesus encouraging them to let their roots grow deep. He knows that we are best suited for depth in relationship and ministry. I have seen people who jump from church to church, always ready to spit out complaints and woes, never satisfied with a ministry or a pastor or a church style. Truthfully, we will never find the perfect church; however, we will find churches with great intentions and a Christ-centered vision. And once we do, we have been asked to become established and sink deep down into our service.

Litter Picker-Uppers: Excellence in Our Service

The staff at Glad Tidings has lunch together once a month. We call it our staff meeting, but I always thought it was more fun than the

9   Nancy Beach, An Hour on Sunday: Creating Moments of Transformation and Wonder (Grand Rapids, MI: Zondervan, 2004).

way that sounded. We would get together for lunch and then engage in an hour-long training and sometimes worship. During one of these luncheon trainings, Pastor Bryan shared a simple ideology he lived by. He talked about the pastor who preceded him, Jim Swank. I remember Pastor Swank from when I was a little girl, and I remember him always being a sharp-dressed guy, very debonair in his attire. He would wear a tie and suit, even on a normal workday. But Pastor Swank had a philosophy that Pastor Bryan adopted as his own. It was this: He would never pass a piece of litter on the ground without picking it up. It is a really simple idea, nothing grand or original, but it said a lot about both of these men. From my year as a secretary at the church, I knew what Pastor Bryan's schedule looked like. He was a heavily sought-out man with a busy schedule and a seemingly endless task list. If anyone on staff earned the right to be exempt from picking up trash, it would be him. Yet he had a personal commitment to serving in this small way.

In the foreword of the book The Starbucks Experience: 5 Principles for Turning Ordinary into Extraordinary, the president of Starbucks writes of a similar mind-set.

> I often start stories about our company and culture with a description of us as the litter-picker-upper type of people. We just naturally stoop down to pick up that gum wrapper or soda can on the sidewalk as we're talking with you about how the kids are doing and what crazy weather we're having. It's not a magic formula for hiring or business success; it's just who we are.

Any Starbucks employee knows what you are referring to if you mention the Green Apron Book. It's a short, illustrated book small enough to fit into their apron pocket so they can keep it with them as they work. The book outlines their core "ways of being." It involves five basic principles: be welcoming, be genuine, be knowledgeable, be considerate, and be involved. But to summarize all of this, Jim Alling just calls it the "litter-picker-upper type of people." I absolutely love this terminology, and I consider it to be a great depiction of someone who embraces excellence. Not in an annoying, overly ambitious sense, but in a raw, caring, life-embracing sense.

Someone who embraces excellence through his or her lifestyle is someone who walks around with a readiness to jump onboard. They make things better just by being around. It doesn't really matter what task they are working on because they are the type to walk into a room and say, "How can I help?" These are four powerful words. Excellence-embracers are going to ask the question and then follow through with full abandon to their newly acquired task.

And these are the types of people you want to be friends with. Jesus must've been a litter-picker-upper type of person. I'm sure of it. We see how He made time for children, which seemed unimportant to many other people. He even said, "I tell you the truth, anyone who will not receive the kingdom of God like a little child will never enter it" (Luke 18:17). We love to overcomplicate matters, and we do that in our service. We even like to believe that serving in big ways is more important than serving in small ways. But to Jesus, both were pretty important.

Another indicator of a litter-picker-upper type of person is that they show not tell. At our church, we always teach our volunteers to take the time to show people an answer rather than tell them an answer. If someone is looking for the bathrooms, the preschool wing, or the Sunday school room, we tell our volunteers to walk them to the room instead of giving them a pile of verbal directions. This is a simple way to move service from good to great, and it also makes people feel like they matter. And if you see a gum wrapper on the floor as you are walking someone to the bathroom, talking about how they're day is going, an excellence-embracer will nonchalantly bend down and pick it up because that's just the type of person he or she is.

Excellence in Our Creativity.

"I saw the angel in the marble and carved until I set him free." Michelangelo[10]

Excellence within the church has a lot to do with our actions, but it also has a lot to do with our creative energies. Art has been depicted through the generations from ancient sketchings to the graffiti on dirty street sidings to the architect's brilliant lines that outline the skies. But arguably the most jaw-dropping art is the immaculate orchestrations that sprawl cathedral ceilings. Stained glass tapestries and marble-carved stories and paintings stun onlookers to silence as they revel in it.

The philosopher Plotinus said, "Art deals with things forever incapable of definition that belong to love, beauty, joy, and worship ..."[11] What is most exciting yet saddening to me is that there was a time when the best art belonged to the churches. Visit Saint Peter's in Rome or Notre Dame in Paris, and you will not need to wonder for long about the artistic influences that reside there. Michelangelo, Raphael, and Bosch's art are all displayed primarily throughout the churches, not the halls of art museums. It is exciting that it was once true and evidenced in its brilliance throughout these structures. However, it is saddening because art, in many ways, has been lost to the church.

> Church buildings were ...beautiful. Whether ornate cathedrals or simple gathering places, these structures were crafted of the finest materials by the world's most

---

10 J. Patrick. Lewis and Buonarroti Michelangelo, *Michelangelo's World* (Mankato, MN: Creative Editions, 2007).

11 Diana Loomans and Julia Loomans, 100 Ways to Build Self-esteem and Teach Values (Tiburon, CA: H J Kramer, 2003).

skilled artisans. The very idea that the arts in church could be anything less than excellent would have been unthinkable to believers in former centuries. So how did we lose our way?[12]

We are not willing to pay the price anymore for excellent creative execution. Perhaps we hardly even recognize its necessity anymore. Because of the nature of what the church is—a gathering with lots of people all pointing to God's goodness—it is bursting with the potential to be an outpouring of creative and artistic representation of God! And creating within the church has a positive influence on the whole attitude of the church. As Paul Angone put it, "Complaining and creating have a direct correlation. The more you create, the less you complain. The more you complain, the less you create. It's a pretty simple formula."[13] I've heard Pastor Bryan say we should be change agents instead of change analysts. It's because when you begin to create, your efforts are engaged. Complaining becomes a frivolous expulsion of time when there is creating to be done.

Recently, I inquired to a Chilean artist about a work of art I wanted to purchase. I have never purchased an original work of art; you know, the one that the artist actually touched. It turns out that it was completely out of my price range. Yet I wasn't surprised by the price tag because this piece was an original. Things of beauty and excellence often come at a high price. And to gain ownership of it, to come into a place of reconciliation with magnificence, involves investment. I think God revels in it when we use the minds, hands, and imaginations He gave us to create things that point back to His beauty.

---

12 Nancy Beach, An Hour on Sunday: Creating Moments of Transformation and Wonder (Grand Rapids, MI: Zondervan, 2004).

13 Paul Angone, "Creativity's Worst Enemy," RELEVANT Magazine, October 10, 2012, section goes here, accessed July 22, 2013, http://www.relevantmagazine.com/next/grow/creativitys-worst-enemy.

In her book, An Hour on Sunday, Nancy Beach writes about raising up artists within the church. She sees its significance. One of her chapters begins with the sentiment, "I sometimes allow myself to dream about what would happen if the church once again became known as a place where outstanding art was created for God."[14] Amidst her thoughts she includes this thought-provoking entry from Frank Schaeffer:

> Of all people, Christians should be addicted to quality and integrity in every area, not looking for excuses for second-best …We must look for people with real creative integrity and talent, or we must not dabble in these creative fields at all. All of this does not mean that there is no room for the first halting steps, for experimentation, for mistakes, and for development. But it does mean that there is no room for lazy, entrenched, year-after-year established mediocrity, unchanging and unvaried.[15]

I appreciate that Schaeffer emphasizes that we should not only "dabble in these creative fields" if we are going to strive for excellence. Notice what he is not saying is that every church must be an aesthetic revolution. Yet there is a basic desire in his statement for the church to reclaim a pursuit of aesthetics. This will look different for different churches, based on the giftings within the church. Some will expound their creative energies on music, stage design, graphic design, acting, writing, and teaching. Some will use these for outreaches within the community or Christmas productions or newsletters. Whatever and however this looks for your church, execute it through excellence.

---

14 Nancy Beach, An Hour on Sunday: Creating Moments of Transformation and Wonder (Grand Rapids, MI: Zondervan, 2004).

15 Rory Noland, The Heart of the Artist: A Character-building Guide for You & Your Ministry Team (Grand Rapids, MI: Zondervan Pub. House, 1999),

Excellence in Our Kindness.

In the fall, I attended a women's conference in Hershey, Pennsylvania. High estrogen levels and an endless supply of chocolate. Need I say more? As part of the staff, I loved seeing the inner workings of the conference and especially interacting with the diverse group of leaders—a selection of authors, speakers, and musicians. On the first night, Ruth gathered together our small leadership team and addressed us with concern. "There will be over twenty-five hundred women here this weekend, which means there will be a lot of needs." Liz Curtis Higgs agreed. "Twenty-five hundred needs," she echoed.

A need looks like many different things—a knotted stomach, a painful memory, hands coming up empty. Needs can either be a bulky presence or a small annoyance, but they never fully dissipate. To think that every woman was bringing one along with her was sobering. Over the convening days, I became acutely aware of the needs as stories began to tumble out. A diagnosis. An approaching court date. A breakup. A job loss. The needs were so large they were crowding our vast meeting hall. What I realized is that our churches, neighborhoods, schools, and workplaces are filled with people, and each one has a deeply felt, very personal need. So how are we going to reach them through our efforts of excellence? Is it ultimately through our excellent programming, the impeccable upkeep of our buildings, or our extravagant funding of community projects? These are all important, but I choose none of these ultimately. No, I think excellence best meets the needs of people when we are excellent with our kindness. Perhaps the best thing we can do is to help ease the pain of the world through our kindness.

Jeff Bezos, the CEO and founder of Amazon, delivered a graduation address to his alma mater, Princeton University. In it, he looked at all of the bright Ivy League students who sat before him, teeming with potential, and told them, "One day you'll understand that it's harder to be kind than clever."[16]

As humans, God has gifted us with the ability to accomplish much, and we have the potential to astound ourselves. And we should strive to sharpen our minds and hone our skills to be the best version of ourselves we can possibly be. "Do not neglect your gifts," we are instructed in 1 Timothy 4:14–15. "Be diligent in these matters; give yourself wholly to them, so that everyone may see your progress."

But kindness? As Bezos explained, looking out into the audience of Princeton grads, kindness is a choice. He acknowledged that each person who sat before him was smart, skilled, and full of potential, yet he chose to address them on the topic of kindness. The point he was making is that kindness is not an endowment to the elite but rather a choice for the masses.

And will we make that choice? Can we be excellent in our kindness to others? To extend kindness in a manner that closely resembles Christ? To be radical in our kind words and actions? Goethe says that we are to "Treat people as if they were what they ought to be, and you will help them to become what they are capable of being."[17] We see Jesus doing this all through the Gospels. He sees people with these great needs, and He goes completely out of His way to act in an elaborately kind manner. And He redeems their life and changes their destiny.

Instructions to Love

When it comes to programming, think ahead, plan, process, and be thorough, but when it comes to people, love without abandon. When

---

16   Jeff Bezos, "What Matters More than Your Talents" (speech, Princeton University Graduation Address), accessed October 25, 2012, http://www. ted.com/talks/jeff_bezos_gifts_vs_choices.html.

17   Michael D. Sabock, Ralph J. Sabock, and Ralph J. Sabock, Coaching: A Realistic Perspective (Lanham, MD: Rowman & Littlefield Publishers, 2011),

dealing with people, which includes most of our encounters, there is oftentimes no protocol. In most cases, excellence in loving people just looks unselfish and vast. There is a story that Bob Goff, author of *Love Does*, tells.

> The woman who lives across the street from us has cancer. She called me up and told me the bad news, and I told her, "I'm not going to call you ever again." She's like, "What?"
>
> I went to Radio Shack and got us two walkie-talkies, and it was terrific. For the last year, we've been talking on walkie-talkies every night. It's like we're both fourteen-year-olds and we're both in tree forts.
>
> She took a turn for the worse about four days ago, so this morning, I woke up about five, and I went to the hospital. I sent the nurse in with a walkie-talkie, and I sat in the next room and called her up. I heard her just start crying—because there's something inefficient and beautiful about it. We were sitting in a hospital, separated by a room, talking on walkie-talkies …
>
> Be inefficient with your love. The more inefficient, the better. It would have been a lot more efficient for God to not send Jesus to die for us. That was very inefficient love. But so sweet and so tender.[18]

Splash

Excellence makes me uncomfortable. There are many reasons it causes me discomfort, but for one, excellence requires an awful lot of work. It requires extra exertion. It inevitably means that I must try

---

18   Bob Goff, "*10 Ways to Live an Extraordinary Life*," Relevant Magazine, Issue 60, November/December 2012, pg. 61.

significantly more than I would for mediocre or average. It means more energy and more resources. And it also means the potential risk of failure. When you try for something with all you've got, you have everything to lose.

So maybe you are hovering just above the waterline that separates mediocre from excellent. Your big toe is edging toward the glittery surface. You're testing it out. And then comes a moment of decision. Will you plunge into these new waters? Oftentimes, mediocrity does not have the courage for excellence. It doesn't have the guts to go for it.

In 2 Kings 8:4, the king instructs the servant, "Tell me about all the great things Elisha has done." Notice how the king did not say, "Please list off all of Elisha's mediocre, halfhearted endeavors" or "Tell me about Elisha's average accomplishments." The king was looking for greatness! He wanted to be wowed.

Don't almost, kind-of, sort-of strive for something; don't be mediocre. If you are going to do something, do it wholeheartedly or don't bother at all. I am young, but I know, even now, that when I look back, I hardly ever remember the mediocre. When I think about the many teachers whose instructions I've sat under, I only remember the painfully awful or the exceptional ones. It is the same with books, films, and vacations. There are many instances of mediocrity that I have completely forgotten. In my own comings and goings, I remember the miserable failures and the victorious wins but not much in between.

Be memorable. Be memorable through your excellence, and as you do, you will leave a lasting impression on others and on God's kingdom. As Bob Goff says, "Don't just put a toe in the water. Do a cannonball with your life!"[19]

---

19   *Love Does, Thanks*, perf. Bob Goff, Www.bobgoff.com, August 10, 2012, http://bobgoff.com/thanks-for-getting-us-on-the-nyt-best-sellers-list/.

Chapter Summary

» Aspiring toward greatness is that small thing inside each one of us that hopes. It is the hope that our lives amount to something.

» View the idea of greatness as both large and small tasks executed with excellence.

» In its search for excellence, every church should aim for a sense of individuality rather than just copying successful programs from other churches.

» Jesus' measurements for greatness are not the same as those used by our world.

» Jesus' road toward greatness is one that is paved by the inefficient marks of sacrifice, surrender, and service.

» Whether service is done poorly or with excellence, it is always a reflection of the larger embodiment of the organization.

» As servants, we are called to reflect the master chef and be the deliverers of sustenance.

» As Christians, we have been called to transcendence, designed to live and reflect the light of a transcendent being.

» Within its walls, the church should tell a story, evoke an emotion, and spur forth something unearthly.

» Our sweat and tears are often the precursors to God's fruitfulness.

» As Christians, let us create a reputation for being hard workers, both within and outside the walls of the church. Let us be a people who companies are eager to hire because we are people famous for our hard work, integrity, and degree of excellence.

» True excellence necessitates follow-through and demands an investment.

» The more you create, the less you complain. The more you complain, the less you create.

» Complaining becomes a frivolous expulsion of time when there is creating to be done.

» In the church, there should be no room for lazy, entrenched, year-after-year established mediocrity.

» "Treat people as if they were what they ought to be, and you will help them to become what they are capable of being." Goethe

Questions

» What if your church was the one place in your community known for rare and excellent service?

» When you have the impulse to serve, what is normally your central hesitation?

» What are the qualities that define excellent, extravagant service for you?

» When have you lavished someone else with excellent service?

» How can the church do a better job within your community in serving extravagantly? How can you help?

» In what area of your life will you commit to serving others with more excellent service?

» How are you striving for excellence in the area of the church where you serve?

Pulled In

Name a state, and I've likely attended a wedding there. I've been to weddings all over the place, from the barns of Pennsylvania to the cliffs of Hawaii, from the vineyards in California to the sun-speckled mountains of Oregon. I've seen weddings of all sizes and color schemes and in all venues—each defined stylistically by the couple about to be hitched. What I love the most about weddings is their ability to bring people together.

The last wedding I attended was in Minnesota. As a bridesmaid, I stayed busy with the pre-wedding festivities. During the prep work, I grew acquainted with the family of the groom, who I hadn't met previously. Totaling seven kids plus the parents, the family was a large group of genuinely good people. The kind of free spirits that put you as ease by their natural well-being and sense of humor. My friend was soon to meld into their family, taking on their name, as she was soon to become a Rouser. After one week with their family, I was endeared, especially to the bright-eyed nine-year-old who attached to my side for the week.

The night of the rehearsal dinner, Sinatra tunes serenaded us throughout the restaurant. I was chatting with the youngest, Cathryn, and told her, "You have a great family. You make me want to be a Rouser!" She looked at me peculiarly. Later that evening, as we sat around the tables digesting our Italian dinner, Cathryn came over and pulled me out of my chair to where the younger cousins were twirling to the big band music. I then became the munchkins' dance partner. At the end of the evening, we were all gathering our belongings to head home when Cathryn came over to me and said, "You're one of us now."

"How?" I said, wondering what had elicited this decisive shift of perspective. "Because we pulled you in!" she said as though it was obvious. She was allocating her approval; I was in. She was saying that by inviting me to the makeshift dance floor, she had given me a tangible invitation, not just to dance, but also to become part of the family. From her simple statement, something dawned on me that I thought about it for the rest of the night. I thought about the good accomplished through the act of being pulled in, through the invitation to become a participant in life.

Ironically, one of the Rouser kids had been pulled in herself. Their seventeen-year-old daughter, Alyssa, was rescued from an unhealthy home situation when she was eleven. Her father had been schizophrenic and her mom was an alcoholic and drug user. Alyssa was adopted by the Rousers and treated like one of their own. I suspect that her future might have turned out very differently had she not been invited into a stable, loving family. I am not elevating their family on a pedestal. No family is perfect, and I am sure they would tell you they are not the exception. However, I bet that God envisions the church to look somewhat like the Rouser family—just a bunch of people who are celebrating something good and inviting others to join them. There is a redemptive quality in a community that joyfully pulls people in—a family in the business of recruitment.

Q: Was there a time when you had been "pulled in" to something good? How did it make you feel?

> After this the Lord appointed seventy-two others and sent them two by two ahead of him to every town and place where he was about to go. He told them, "The harvest is plentiful, but the workers are few. Ask the Lord of the harvest, therefore, to send out workers into his harvest field." (Luke 10:1–2)

God Pulls Us In

At the start of Luke 10, Jesus pulls in and recruits a large number of people—seventy-two to be exact—for the purpose of readying the townspeople for His arrival into their hometown. Can you imagine the excitement of joining the movement of Jesus in the flesh? You would have been witnessing His miracles and hearing His teachings. Then consider the elation when you were asked to take part in this rising momentum! The first time we see Jesus recruit others to ministry is when He designates the twelve disciples as His core followers. The second occurs when Jesus recruits this large number of volunteers for a specific purpose. Jesus asks them to join in His service, which is pretty amazing when you consider that God in the flesh is recruiting human help. One who was completely capable without extra assistance chose to include us.

He freely chose us and has done so through adoption, establishing His relationship with us, and through appointing, which establishes the task at hand. We will look at these two modes of recruitment before we dive into how it relates to our service. To give you a foretaste of where we are headed, to serve is inevitably to recruit. But in order to recruit, we must see plainly that we have been recruited ourselves. Ultimately, this open-door policy of recruitment is the reason why Christ and the church are the hope of the world.

A Secular Look at Recruitment

When you hear the word recruit, I doubt you think about church or spiritual growth. Most likely the word evokes ties to familiar establishments within our society. Recruitment is affiliated with the military services like the army or navy. Another affiliation is among athletes, where the most adept players are recruited to play for a particular sports team. Tons of agencies hire employees for the purpose of recruiting in the name of their organization—scouts search far and wide for the best athletes, producers search for hidden musical talent on YouTube and beyond, and admissions counselors open and close the gate of admission to their school or university. Corporations recruit for a business deal or for affiliates in a partnership. Name an institution, and most likely it recruits in some form or another.

Since childhood, we have been familiar with the concept of recruitment. Remember as a kid waiting to be picked for a neighborhood kickball team? Those long, drawn-out minutes of standing in line, holding your breath, and hoping your name would be the next one called? Each kid was secretly envious of the first player picked. And as the captain shouted name after name, recruitment after recruitment, there was the growing dread that your name would be the last one called.

Since we were youngsters, we have been aware that there are competitive systems in place, and we silently hope we are not left out of them. We watched our dad or mom go through layoffs or promotions. We saw the evolution of the popular crowds in school who had their own lunch tables and their own parties to which everyone on the outside desired inclusion. There are billions of ways that can be defined within our culture, but it always necessitates a process of elimination with an obvious choosing of some and eliminating of others. Either a nomination or a disqualification.

This constant streamlining and narrowing down sets the standards for which we are evaluated. We emerge into the rat race of life, each eagerly hoping to be recruited to the next big thing. So begins the exhaustive and competitive process, which to recruitment means to choose, appoint, and adopt but only an elite few. And this is how mankind took something that Jesus laid the foundation for— recruitment—and turned it sideways, as we so often do. We corrupted the good found in being chosen, incorporated, and included and turned it into a ladder to climb instead of a doorway to enter.

It is a tireless state; however, there is good news. Jesus opened the door. He let us in and instated us into a system that offers acceptance, identity, and purpose. First Peter 2:9 declares, "But you are a chosen people, a royal priesthood, a holy nation, God's special possession." In this, we can claim our place in the world.

Q: How has competition and striving impacted you (within your career, hobbies, relationships?)

Recruitment as Adoption

I was one of the lucky few raised in a stable home. There wasn't a ton of arguing, my parents never threatened divorce or went to bed angry, or any of those scenarios that cause people to become jaded as they grow up. In most counseling sessions or psychological circles, any kind of analysis normally leads to the prominent topical pit stop of "daddy issues." The term itself has gained an ominous notoriety. It is the buzzword of counseling sessions, confronting the private issues no one used to talk about. It's us looking back as informed adults to identify that our father's (or mother's) abandonment, absence, coddling, etc. left a huge, whopping dent somewhere in our unconscious. Here we are, as grown men and women, wobbling about with these gaping ruts in our path, slowing our journey toward becoming whole, healthy individuals. At least that's what the experts say. We have been prominently defined by our "daddy issues."

Although I don't altogether counter these conclusions, I disagree that the outcome of each person should derive solely from the effects of his or her father's or mother's behavior. There is, however, an aspect that I readily grab hold of: the notion that we all draw our identity from a foundational base, which is the source of our view of self, perspectives about life, and ideas for our future. It is the home base, our mother ship, on which we are formed and created in likeness. If we latch onto the thought that our biological father (or mother) deserves credit (or blame) for our ultimate outcome, we are doomed to fail, for no human being should be entirely responsible for the outcome of another human being. But there is one exception. If there existed a perfect father who distinctly imprinted upon his children the right way to act, words to say, and how to think, the whole idea of "daddy issues" would be immaterial.

By now you have probably assumed the case I am formulating. We can have a healthy relationship with our heavenly Father who does not leave us scarred by "daddy issues." We will not be burned by the poor decisions of His actions. We will not be messed up by the learning curve of parenting in relevance to God. This Father, with a capital F, does, in fact, exist. And He craves relationship with each of His children. Whether you have managed to escape childhood relatively unscathed or were dramatically wounded by the car wreck that is your family, this perfect fatherhood is an adoption agency. It is a canopy that offers its services to any who wish to dwell beneath it.

So how we do come into this son or daughter relationship with the creator of the universe? How do we connect through familial ties to a vast creator? How do we transition our thinking from biological ownership to ownership of a heavenly realm? It sounds mythical like we are referring to Hercules rather than Christendom. Or naïve, like we are all little redheads and God is the Daddy Warbucks of the world. Yet this idea of God as father is truthful and pivotal. The only way we can understand this fatherhood is through the knowledge of what is promised to us through Scripture. Repeatedly in the Word, God is referred to as "Father" or "Abba Father," and we are told that we are His offspring. In Romans, it says that we "received the Spirit of sonship (or adoption.) And by him we cry, 'Abba Father.' The Spirit himself testifies with our spirit that we are God's children" (Romans 8:15–16). What an odd principle to grasp—that we have been adopted. Our name has been changed. Our identity is redefined.

In Sunday school, we would sing, "Father Abraham had many sons. And many sons had father Abraham. And I am one of them. And so are you. So lets just praise the Lord. Right arm ...left arm ..."[1] And the song would continue until we all looked a bit nutty, flailing our arms and legs and yelling about our sonship to this guy named Abraham from the Bible. Heartily and with gusto, we sang about our spiritual lineage. As kids, we readily grasped hold of the concept of being adopted into the kingdom of God. Although we sang the song with enthusiasm, I wonder if we downplayed the importance of the words we were singing. The promise of our adoption only has significance when we come face-to-face with the angst of our orphaned nature.

Q: Has your "daddy/mommy issues" affected the way you view God? If so, in what way(s)?

"X" Marks the Spot

Somewhere along the way, we have all been displaced. What I mean is that our roots, the part of us that felt safe and secure, were yanked

---

1   Cedarmont Kids, "Father Abraham," in *Action Bible Songs*, Cedarmont Music, 1995, MP3.

out from underneath us. For some of us, it was the roots of identity or the roots of feeling loved, but what we once had, we lost along the way. We were left as orphans in a place of depravity.

Jon Acuff writes about a night in Pensacola, Florida, when he walked into a BP gas station. At checkout, there was a haggard-looking woman behind the counter. He described her as "tired, like maybe life was hard for her a decade too soon …On the outside of her hand was a small greenish-gray tattoo of an X." Upon seeing the scribbly tattoo, he was curious and asked her about it. She told him it was nothing, that when she was thirteen, her mom was drunk and tattooed it onto her hand. That unsettled Jon. He thought about what that must have been like "showing up to school one Monday with a jagged, bloody green X tattooed on your hand? What was that experience like? How would kids react to that? Didn't it hurt when her mom gave her that? She was drunk, writing on her daughter with a shaky hand and a hot needle."[2] Jon's wondered about the different ways we are marked by parents, coworkers, strangers, even ourselves.

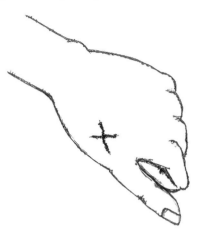

Over time, though, our hands grow calloused and the marks remain and multiply. What was once the presence of innocence becomes redefined and weathered. Can't you sense it as you grow older? Awareness of hardship darkens the lines on your face. It adds a sad depth to your eyes. The marks tattooed onto us from grief, debt,

2   Jon Acuff, "The Little Girl's Tattoo.," Stuff Christians Like, April 18, 2012, section goes here, accessed July 22, 2013, http://www.jonacuff.com/ stuffchristianslike/2012/04/the-little-girls-tattoo/.

divorce, sickness, and jabbing comments that told us we were ugly, fat, or stupid leave us feeling alone and deprived. We hunger for love. We hunger to be reclaimed and embraced. If that is not the image of an orphan, I ask you, what is?

Once we see ourselves as orphans, the guarantee of our adoption is life-giving. Jesus compassionately approaches us and promises, "I will not leave you as orphans; I will come to you" (John 14:18). And then he pulls us in for our rescue.

Q: What marks have you allowed to stick? How have they shaped the person you are?

Q: How would your life be different if those marks were erased? What would freedom from your marks look like?

I'm Adopted

In the first century, the laws concerning adoption were rather peculiar. We tend to think that a biological child has a stronger bond to the family than an adopted child, affirming that the adopted child is secondary. However, according to Roman law, the bonds of adoption were stronger than that of biological ties, as it was permissible for a father to disown his biological children, but under Roman law, it was impossible to disown an adopted child. Additionally, any past debt of the adopted was completely canceled, and the status of the new family carried over to them as well. Adoption was one way for a slave to rise in status. When we read in Paul's letters statements like "you are no longer a slave, but a son; and since you are a son, God has made you also an heir" (Galatians 4:7), we see the huge ramifications within that culture. Adoption encompassed freedom and a literal newness of personhood. In other words, adoption was a big deal. Think about it ...a biological son could be estranged, but an adopted son could not be separated from his father. Parallel that to Jesus' separation from His father on behalf of our adoption! Adoption is an incredible way to look at the way God wants to establish relationship with us.

With a more thorough understanding of our adoption through Christ, we can trace it back to the concept of recruitment. As mentioned earlier, Jesus recruited all peoples of the world through His adoption. A few of the definitions for the verb recruit have a curious semblance to adoption. To recruit is to gain new supplies of anything lost or wasted, to renew or restore, to recover health, strength, and spirits. [3]

Without stretching the imagination, these descriptions closely resemble the actions of a father who is an agent of adoption. A father who is feverishly aching to find the one who has been lost or wasted; yearns to return the orphan back to health, strength, and spirit; and has the ability to renew and restore. It is a beautiful, restorative image of recruitment. When we understand the kind of goodness and grace that flows out of the idea of God as father, it changes everything. It depicts a God who is in pursuit of us, who wants to recruit us in a deeply relational manner. It gives us a glimpse into His heart, which is bent toward compassionate adoption. Donald Miller puts it like this:

I think there are a lot of religious trends that would have us controlling God, telling us that if we do this and that and another, God jumps through our hoops like a monkey. But this other God, this real God, is awesome and strong, all-encompassing and passionate, and for reasons I will never understand, He wants to father us. [4]

Q: What was your adoption by the heavenly Father like?

---

3   The American Heritage Dictionary of the English Language, 5th ed. (Boston, MA: Houghton Mifflin Harcourt Trade, 2011), s.v. "Recruit."

4   Donald Miller, *Father Fiction: Chapters for a Fatherless Generation* (Nashville, TN: Howard Books, 2010), pg. 67.

The Whisper Test:
A Story Told by Mary Ann Bird

"I grew up knowing I was different, and I hated it. I was born with a cleft palate, and when I started school, my classmates made it clear to me how I looked to others: a little girl with a misshapen lip, crooked nose, lopsided teeth, and garbled speech.

"When schoolmates asked, 'What happened to your lip?' I'd tell them I'd fallen and cut it on a piece of glass. Somehow it seemed more acceptable to have suffered an accident than to have been born different. I was convinced that no one outside my family could love me.

"There was, however, a teacher in the second grade whom we all adored—Mrs. Leonard by name. She was short, round, happy—a sparkling lady.

"Annually, we had a hearing test. Mrs. Leonard gave the test to everyone in the class, and finally it was my turn. I knew from past years that as we stood against the door and covered one ear, the teacher sitting at her desk would whisper something, and we would have to repeat it back—things like 'The sky is blue' or 'Do you have new shoes?' I waited there for those words that God must have put into her mouth, those seven words that changed my life. Mrs. Leonard said in her whisper, 'I wish you were my little girl.'"

If we listen for God's intentional whisper, we will find that He is telling us the same message. And in the same way that it redefined Mary's life, it could radically redefine yours as well.

Recruit Those Left as Orphans
Hopeless. Dreary. Alone.

Dreams were suffocated in this place. Joy was choked out. All was bleak. The orphanage was cold, and the gray walls enclosed the gloom. Dust outlined the windows, mirrors, and furniture. Small children, the motherless and fatherless, walked down the hallways in silent lines. The procession of the unwanted. Life had drained out of them like a river thinned out after a long drought. Their one concession was the gift of one another. A mutual misery bonded them together. Orphan beside orphan, their loneliness was endowed with a companion. Their hidden longing was captured within the hearts of one another, espousing an apathy that could only coincide with shared pain.

But one day, as the orphans are seated around a long wooden table over breakfast, the door squeaks open. The matron walks in and calls out your name. You stand up reluctantly. Might you dare to hope? She leads you to her office and sits you down. She tells you the words you hoped would someday come: You have been selected for adoption. You are being relinquished from this prison. You are being set free to start afresh.

Weeks later, you have settled in with your new family, and life has never been better. Your demeanor has changed, for life has entered you again. Your eyes and cheeks bear a smile. You are discovering love for the first time in a safe, warm environment. Through the transition from orphanage to home, you knew the living conditions would improve, but you did not fathom the depth of renewal your soul would encounter. The feeling of belonging is a gift that exceeds any outside comforts. However, there is a slight uneasiness that unnerves you. Despite efforts to unfasten yourself from the dreariness of the orphanage, it trespasses through your mind as you sleep. The faces of your fellow orphans—your friends, the unrescued—are imprinted upon you. And you yearn for their adoption. You desperately wish they could know the warmth of a home. The peace of a family. The confidence of a future. You wish you could reach them.

Although you might not think this is your story, it is your story, or at least it should be. Since we have come to know Christ who has rescued us from our orphaned past, we have been moved from gloom and doom to a place of belonging. If you have not been reminded of the greatness of this in a while, let me remind you now. GOOD NEWS: YOU BELONG.

This new state births an understanding within us that someone greater has claimed ownership of us and changes us from within. But the sad part of the story is that there are still orphans. What about those who remain? Have you wondered about those people—the ones who still lack roots? Does your heart yearn to lead those who are still orphans to freedom? Do you desperately wish they could be recruited into God's family? We normally tag the word evangelism to this concept. We say, "Go evangelize in the name of Jesus," and technically, this message should stir you up. But I suspect the church has grown immune to it. So I am rephrasing it. Go recruit the orphans to God's family.

Oftentimes, when we move into our salvation through Jesus, we are so avid to leave everything from our past behind us that we also abandon the people who are associated with it. As the saying goes, we like to throw the baby out with the bath water. Those who have not yet discovered that Christ desires them live recklessly. We were all at that place once. "At that time you were separate from Christ, excluded from citizenship in Israel and foreigners to the covenants of the promise, without hope and without God in the world" (Ephesians 2:12). But through our restitution, we become new in the attitudes of our minds (Eph. 4:23) so we are anxious to leave our reckless habits and behaviors behind us. Of course Jesus advocates for this newness to be evidenced through our lives, yet He distinctly asks us not to leave people behind. He wants us to recruit them into the family as well.

In the gospel of John, we hear Jesus' metaphor, "I have other sheep that are not of this sheep pen. I must bring them also. They too will listen to my voice, and there shall be one flock and one shepherd" (John 10:16). Jesus' words are a demonstration of what was mentioned earlier: Jesus' plan of recruitment encompasses all people. He does not pick and choose who He desires and then sits back in satisfaction, saying, "I think we have enough now. We are filled to capacity." No. None are excluded. It is an open-door policy. To take it a step further, He chooses to use those who have already been adopted as His recruitment tool. He asks that we remember the orphans—the sheep without a shepherd—and invite them into his kingdom. It is our responsibility, the job with the highest priority, to seek out people who lack hope and point them in the right direction.

Later in this chapter, we are going to delve into the adventures of engaging people into church, ministry, and service, but our primary purpose is to recruit them into the kingdom. Sometimes inviting people to church can be a great segue into their adoption, but it is essential that we do not excuse ourselves from the process. It should become our personal initiative and passion rather then merely sending out church invites and letting the pastor take it from there. Each of us is personally invited to invest in those who are still orphans.

Q: When in your life was your heart broken for spiritual orphans?

Oftentimes, as Christ-followers, we live in light of eternity but remain ignorant to the consequences of eternal death. Perhaps we do not realize that this life we are living has an undetermined deadline, which is horrific news for those who do not know Christ. Loneliness and dwindling is normally slow and goes unnoticed; therefore, we lack urgency in our response to it. We must be urgent and fervent about sharing the good news of a saving Father with the orphans we encounter. C. S. Lewis shares, "The safest road to hell is the gradual one—the gentle slope, soft underfoot, without sudden turnings, without milestones, without signposts."[5] Do not dawdle or dwindle when it comes to sharing the good news of the gospel with people. Instead, be an agent of change within the lives of the people around you! Remember that you were first adopted and can now guide others to God the Father's loving embrace. Let them also experience the deep joy of being pulled in like a weathered fishermen who pulls in his net at the end of the day.

Q: Why do you sometimes neglect Jesus' message of evangelism? How can you change this?

Appointment: The Transition into Service

Hopefully, you fully grasp that you have been recruited through your adoption. Now what? The door has been opened, and you walked through it. So what waits on the other side? It is time to take on a role within your new family. Each member of a family has a specific role. There is a father, mother, son, daughter, cousin, uncle, and so on, and each has a place and purpose within the family unit that adds color, personality, and vitality to the family.

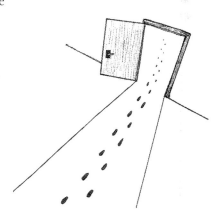

So the second part of recruitment is appointment, which is where you are assigned a role within the family. In Luke 10:1, the word appoint describes Jesus' action. He "appointed

---

5   C. S. Lewis and Walter Hooper, *Christian Reflections* (Grand Rapids: W.B. Eerdmans Pub., 1967).

seventy-two others and sent them two by two ahead of him to every town and place where He was about to go."[6] This is where the action starts. Our adoption was great news, the game changer! Our adoption was the inciting incident that caused forward motion. But the appointment is when the adventures of this new family lifestyle begin to take shape. In the Greek, appointed is anadeiknumi, which literally means, "to proclaim anyone as elected to office; to announce as appointed a king, general, etc; to lift up anything on high and exhibit for all to behold."[7] Sounds impressive, doesn't it? To be appointed is clearly depicted as a notable recognition of a new role. Most likely there were feasts, celebrations, and first-century paparazzi. The description of appointed procures that a position of significance is being filled.

Now consider the connotations of the word serving. Serving is most often associated with lowering yourself in position, status, or mentality. Therefore, a clear contradiction exists between appointing and serving. Yet this passage of Scripture insinuates that they are interchangeable. Jesus appoints seventy-two volunteers to serve. What Jesus does here is key: He is challenging us to rearrange our preconceived notions about the least and the greatest among us.

However, what Jesus is not doing is manipulating us through His rhetoric into working for Him without pay. First, the price Jesus paid when He forgave us from the wrath of sin and death is far beyond any efforts of reimbursement. Secondly, Jesus knew that our hearts would draw closest to the heart of the Father's if we were serving. And in that sense, drawing closer to the Father's heart was the best position to which He could recruit.

---

6   Luke 10:1

7   Thayer and Smith. *"Greek Lexicon Entry for Anadeiknumi."* "The NAS New Testament Greek Lexicon". 1999.

"This" Is Actually "That"

Oftentimes, we take ourselves far too seriously. We crave recognition and yearn for status, wealth, happiness, and comfort. However, Jesus does not treasure these things, which is where the disconnect forms between His message and our understanding. For Him to compare service to kingship seems infinitely skewed. Yet when we serve, the things we treasure alter. What once held importance and weight shifts entirely.

Have you ever noticed that when you are trudging through a difficult time, such as wrestling with grief, loss, or heartache, that the trivial matters of life shrink in comparison to the enormity of your internal pain? In those dark moments, I found that I drew nearer to God more than I would if all had been well. In those sorrow-filled times when I was desperate for escape, retrospect reveals how my difficulties spurred on surrender of my will and deepened my reliance on God. Looking backward, I admit that the growth of my character that occurred within the pain was indeed worth it. What God says to you and me in those times is this, "What you think is My best, such as safety, security, and the absence of pain, is not truly the best I have to offer. Instead, I offer you goodness, kindness, faithfulness, mercy, love, joy, peace, patience, and an abandonment of self as you grab hold of Me, for I am the almighty, completely capable and compassionate God." He tells us that what we thought was "this" was actually "that." What we thought was pain was actually joy. And what we thought was lowly service was actually an honorable appointment into a higher position.

In relationship to our discussion, Jesus is equating service and appointment for a purpose. When He appointed the seventy-two to travel and prepare others for the arrival of the Messiah, do not assume it was an easy yes on their part. Perhaps they were terrified of the townspeople's reactions. Consider what those seventy-two volunteers were leaving behind to obey Jesus' appointed task. What were the risks involved, and what were they abandoning for Christ's sake? But these concerns were small compared to the grand scheme of a Father who was teaching His children the best possible way to live.

Q: What do you associate with the word serving? What do you associate with the word appointing? Think of a time you have done both, and discuss how each made you feel.

Did being appointed make you feel special? Was it a lot of pressure? When you were serving, did you enjoy it? What did it teach you?

Purpose, Community, and the Bigger Picture

Through our adoption and appointment, we have clearly been recruited into a great position. Now it is time to put legs on our understanding and observe the specifics of our calling.

Inside and Outside the Church Walls

It is important to acknowledge that there are many contexts for service inside and outside of the church. Opportunities exist everywhere. If your son or daughter plays soccer, you could recruit other parents to help with the halftime snacks. If you live near a soup kitchen or a food drive, you could recruit your friends to help box food items every weekend. A friend recruited me to get involved with FREE, an anti-trafficking organization in Reading. Finding a passion oriented in service and recruiting others to join the cause is incredible! Passion is contagious. When we become passionate about anything service-related—such as serving at a shelter, nursing home, little league, or foster care—it provides a chance for us to follow Jesus' model of adopting and appointing. With that said, for the remainder of this chapter, we will focus on recruitment within the church and its roles in ministry. However, the same principles apply whether you are recruiting others to serve within the church or the community.

The church is bursting with volunteer slots just waiting to be filled. As a pastor's kid, I would travel from church to church when my dad would guest speak. Even then, I noticed that every church differed in decor, song choice, and personality, but overall, each consisted of the same basic components. Every church had a kids' ministry. Every church had a media team, whether it consisted of a projector or a few LCD screens. Every church had a music ministry. Regardless of the church, I was never incredibly surprised by the system in which it functioned. From choir to maintenance, housekeeping to age-related ministries, small groups and more, there never seemed to be a shortage of volunteer positions within a church. What I loved to see was people passionate about their ministries. If someone cared about what they did, it was obvious. There was a church that hosted a potluck after the service, and the chef who was hosting it loved to cook and was thrilled to share her talent with the church family. At a church outside of Philly, I remember a guy who led a small kids' ministry. He was so enthusiastic about it that his volunteer team exemplified the same kind of energy. People getting plugged in to serve and appointed into a position brings the body of Christ to life with all of its functioning pieces. It changes the idea of church from the mind-set of "the church" to "my church." Involvement assigns personal purpose to members of the family where it is no longer "the family" but "my family."

Removing Our Anonymity through Purpose

Purpose is a weird thing to define. Pastor Bryan sometimes talks about the trivial nature of life and death with the facts. "We live, we eventually die, and we're buried," he says. "Then afterward, everyone comes back to the church to eat potato salad." The church laughs because we all know that it's true. He is not trying to make life sound insignificant, but truly and honestly, life is fairly unpredictable and fleeting. Even in Scripture, David expresses, "Remember how fleeting is my life. For what futility you have created all men!" (Psalm 89:47). Futility means useless, pointless, or vain.[8] In this remark from the book of Psalms, David sounds like he is dwelling on how pointless, strange, and saddening life can be. "What is the point?" is the question we have all asked ourselves. When we find ourselves questioning our purpose in life, God has an answer and reveals it to us through our service.

In the Gospels, we learn about the twelve disciples by watching their actions and hearing their conversations. We learn about their motives and their heart. As readers, we feel like we are acquainted with them. We get the feel for who they were, what they were like, and can even determine if we would have liked them or not. Peter was headstrong. James and John were competitive. Judas was greedy. Thomas was doubtful. And Matthew was a tax collector. Need I say more? Yet we can relate to all of them. The disciples help launch us into the biblical world that is so far removed from our own. This group of twelve men helps us to walk through the Gospels so that we see aspects of ourselves in relation to Jesus. But when Jesus recruits the seventy-two, we know absolutely nothing about them. Zilch. Zero. Their identities are completely anonymous. We don't know about their past occupations, their favorite hobbies, the names of their donkeys, their lineages … nothing. All we know about them is that they said yes to Jesus' call to service. What I like about them is that their entire significance was defined by their appointment into service. They would have remained nameless and lived and died without record of their existence, but by choosing to serve, their anonymity was erased. They were forever included in the Word of God. Why? Because they gained purpose through their service.

The BIG Question

At Glad Tidings, we host "SERVE Trainings," where new volunteers are educated about the SERVE acronym and how it plays

8   The American Heritage Dictionary of the English Language, 5th ed. (Boston, MA: Houghton Mifflin Harcourt Trade, 2011), s.v. "Futility."

out in ministry. Debbie Bube, who heads up volunteer recruitment and placement, explains how new volunteers are always asked the question, "At the end of your life, what is the one thing you wish to have really made a difference?" For some, they might say they want to help older people feel loved and cared for. Others might say they want to provide kids with a role model because they never had one. Answers will differ, but ultimately, their answers will help guide their placement in service. Debbie wants to recruit as many people as possible to serve because she recognizes that the church cannot function from staff alone. Volunteers are essential to grow a church. Still, she and the rest of the SERVE leadership team are aware that growing the church is not the primary purpose for serving. Debbie shares, "The primary purpose of serving is not to fill all of our roles so that church can function, but it is so people can find their purpose." It is pivotal for a church to relinquish its desire for the church to prosper in exchange for the desire that its congregants believe that their lives fit into the redemptive plan God has for the world. One of our heavily invested volunteers, Tom Readdy, said, "We have all been created with a purpose, and oftentimes, we sit there, trying to figure out what that purpose is. But until we actually start taking the steps to serve, we may not know what it is. But God does. And He meets us right at that place. Next thing we know, we are cruising along, and we know, 'God, this is why You made me.'"

Q: At the end of your life, what is the one way you hope to make a difference?

Find Your Sweet Spot

When you hear the name Albert Einstein, you probably think of two identifiers. One, he was a crazy-looking guy, and two, he was pure genius. His ingenuity largely impacted the world of science, but he must have had a deep understanding of people as well, for he once said, "Everyone is a genius, but if you judge a fish by its ability to climb a tree, it will live its whole life believing that it is stupid."[9] Too often, people lack purpose because they live like fish out of water, neglecting the God-given gifts and skills that God made for them. At Glad Tidings, we like to call it a person's "sweet spot."[10] The sweet spot is the place where you come alive. What wakes you up? What stirs up passion within your being? Is it painting, building, hiking, traveling, writing, or speaking? Is it hosting a dinner party? Is it playing sports? What is it that lights you up? When you discover what that thing is, you can normally trace your gifts from that source. We work best in ministry when we are serving within our gifts and talents.  Andy Stanley phrased it nicely when he said, "My fully exploited strengths are of far greater value to the kingdom than my marginally improved weaknesses."[11] God knows that when we are serving in our most fitting environment, our ministries are likely to exude the natural passion and joy that flows from within us.

Finding our sweet spot in ministry is important because it allows us to hone our gifts and most benefit the church. However, we should push back against the tendency to serve only within our sweet spot, for this negates the attitude of selflessness. Jesus was a great biblical model of this. When we observe His spiritual gifts, we see that He was clearly working within His sweet spot in ministry. Jesus was an excellent teacher. He had excellent people skills. He displayed

9   Matthew Kelly, *The Rhythm of Life: Living Every Day with Passion and Purpose* (New York: Fireside Books, 2004).

10 Max Lucado, *Cure for the Common Life: Living in Your Sweet Spot* (Nashville, TN: W Pub. Group, 2005).

11 *Catalyst Dallas*, perf. Andy Stanley, Www.catalystspace.com, August 19, 2011, http://www.youtube.com/watch?v=SBC7P9OvpUA.

wisdom and discernment. He was devoted to intercessory prayer. Yet when He congregated together with His disciples, how did He serve? He washed their feet. Not because He excelled in foot washing, but because He humbled Himself enough to lead through selfless service.

Q: What are some of your passions and gifts?

Q: What are some possible "sweet spots" for you to serve?

Westernized culture places much emphasis on defining our purpose by what we do from nine to five. In others words, our professional life supposedly defines our purpose. However, in a culture where unemployment is rising and "preference" in relation to occupation is not always our luxury, relying on our job as a source of purpose or utilization of our gifts is precarious. So the question is, how can we embrace the other hours, the hours outside of our vocation, to find fulfillment? For instance, if you work as a bus driver but have incredible skills as an artist, you are not doomed to allow your artistic drive to waste away into the abyss of eternity (with the emotion that only an artist could brandish). God has not determined that we be defined by what we do between nine and five. He is incredibly concerned by how we conduct ourselves in our work and how we handle people as well as by our work ethic. But He never instructed us to find a job and meld our entire life's purpose from it. If you are someone who has suffered from job loss, discontent, lack of success, or dullness in relation to your profession, release yourself from the idea that this defines you because it simply doesn't. Your paycheck is not a truthful indicator of your worth. Once you grasp this truth, you will experience great freedom to use your God-given skills in numerous capacities during the other hours, the hours outside of the nine-to-five slot. It is the difference between making a life and making a living.

Harvest Is Plentiful

You can imagine that Jesus was thrilled when He recruited seventy-two workers to serve. It sounds like a huge number of volunteers, a number that any pastor or ministry leader would be ecstatic to have on board within their church! However, it was a small amount compared to the task at hand. Jesus informs his seventy-two disciples, "The harvest is plentiful but the workers are few" (Luke 10:2). By "the harvest is plentiful," Jesus was acknowledging that people were ripe for hearing good news. They were ready for rescue. But who would help lead them there? He was informing his servants that there was a relentless call for more workers within the kingdom and within the church. Although Jesus was aware of the religious people who kept to their temples and praised with empty words, He was on the search for servants willing to get their hands dirty.

He was looking for normal people like you and me to tirelessly surrender ourselves to a higher calling—one of recruitment. Friends, recognize that you have been recruited and are also a recruiter. You have been adopted and also appointed. You have been assigned to the role of joyfully pulling people in. Paul writes, "The one may be overpowered. Two can defend themselves. A cord of three strands is not quickly broken" (Ephesians 4:12). As a family who has been seized into the arms of a loving Father, we can celebrate, for our individual roles have found placement within this expansive community of believers.

Bryan's Story

The stories of our lives hardly ever unfold in a linear manner. There are many unforeseen detours and curvy, bumpy, sometimes hazardous roads that we must take to reach our destinations. Our lead pastor, Bryan Koch, has been the spiritual leader for our congregation since I was a kid running around the rooms of our felt-boarded Sunday school rooms. For as far back as I can recall, Bryan has been in ministry and active as pastor at Glad Tidings. According to me, this is how it has always been. But Bryan lived a very different life before joining our small church in Reading, Pennsylvania. So twenty years later, there I sat in his office, hearing his complete story.

The quintessential dream of every young, wide-eyed boy is to make it someday and be great. When I was a kid, I dreamed of many grand things. I thought of becoming a dolphin-trainer, and at another age, a carpenter so I could build beautiful things from my imagination. Another time, I hoped to be the owner of Disney. For a winsome child, the sky is the limit. Boys' wishes are different but just as vast. When Bryan was young, like so many other boys, he dreamed of becoming a professional baseball player. He loved the sport, and his father nurtured that love with hours of throwing the ball around in the backyard. From the age of four, Bryan got acquainted with the feel of a baseball in his hands and the rush of a strong throw and a firm catch. He started to practice and play, and his love for the game expanded as he pursued it with vigor.

At the end of one of his high school games, Bryan stood by the on-deck circle, undoing his shin guards, when he heard an unfamiliar voice say his name. He looked up, startled to see a major league baseball scout standing before him. The scout had come to watch another player but was impressed by Bryan, who had played well. This was his first encounter like this, but there were many more to follow.

With a high school diploma in hand, the drafts for the professional teams were scheduled for the day after graduation. Waiting in his parent's house, the clock hands ticked noisily as Bryan waited for the phone to ring. So many hopes were wrapped up in one phone call. And finally, the phone alerted him to attention. Answering, he listened intently until the long-awaited words were spoken. Bryan had been drafted to play for the Chicago White Sox. He had been recruited to play professional baseball!

We will fast-forward the story, but know that the years Bryan played baseball were good years, rich in excitement and spiritual growth. The experiences guided Bryan from a young man to maturity. But his depth of personhood came from a different experience. Depth of character hardly ever evolves from happy times but rather from darkness. During one of his baseball games, Bryan was hit in the eye with a baseball while he was hitting. And the darkness came.

Six months after Bryan's injury, he arrived in Chicago to visit a well-known eye doctor. Bryan hoped the doctor would guide his recovery so he could return to the sport and commence with his life. The last half-year had been a humbling experience dealing with the helplessness of a handicap and the fear of an uncertain future. With a patch covering his swollen eye, he walked into the clinic, anxious to hear the doctor's appraisal. After a thorough examination, the doctor's words engulfed him and his baseball dreams when the doctor told him that he would never play ball again. Numb, Bryan left the office, and when he was finally alone, he cried a deep guttural cry, the kind that emits from us only when our closely held dreams and hopes have been dashed.

The immediate heaviness eventually lessened. Bryan began going through the motions of living, and soon enough, he was alive again. He enrolled in college, pursued accounting, and thought to himself, "If I can't pursue my own dream, I'll pursue the American dream." It was an unusual chapter in his life as he began reconfiguring his future without baseball as an option. But he also lacked the drive for anything else. College offered a significantly different pace than the baseball field, but he was a good student who did well in school. During his second year in college, a small but significant event changed his course once again.

Bryan walked into the chapel service, which was a part of his routine at the small Christian college he attended. When he sat down in chapel, he was unaware that his response to the message that day would impact his life yet again. During the service, Bryan received his call to full-time ministry. This time it wasn't the White Sox calling but God Himself. He heard God's "recruitment" in that moment. After the strenuous journey of the previous few years, Bryan finally heard God through a small whisper, saying, "If you let me, I'll use your life."

And God did. And that is where I become familiar with Bryan's story because it is when he moved into full-time ministry as a pastor. After attending Bible school, Bryan came on staff at Glad Tidings and worked alongside my dad in ministry. Now Bryan serves as a pastor who disciples countless people in their spiritual journey through his teaching and direction. As I listened to Bryan's story, I wondered about the many lives he has impacted through his pastoral ministry. I questioned if his impact would have been as direct in a baseball career. And although I hesitate to credit God for Bryan's eye injury, I cannot help but agree that, ultimately, it was best. And God must've known that too. It was not clear to Bryan when he lost the sight in his eye, nor obvious to him after he was stripped of his passion. In those dark times, Bryan came face-to-face with the pain of un-recruitment.

God stayed silent for a long time, for an uncomfortably long time, until Bryan was finally at a place where his pain could be used for good. And what he learned was that once the wreckage of our failed pursuits settle and our brokenness is in the healing stages, God whispers our recruitment through our private pain, often specifically to where He wants us.

Chapter Summary

» The guarantee of our adoption into the family of God is life-giving.

» A proper image of our heavenly Father depicts a God who is in pursuit of us and wants to recruit us in a deeply relational manner.

» Good News: You belong to the family of God.

» We have been rescued as orphans so that we can rescue others into the family of God.

» Each of us is personally invited to invest in those who are still orphans.

» "The safest road to hell is the gradual one." C. S. Lewis

» Jesus is challenging us to rearrange our preconceived notions about the least and the greatest.

» People getting plugged in to serve and appointed into position brings the body of Christ to life.

» "The primary purpose of serving is not to fill all of our roles so that church can function, but it is so people can find their purpose." Deb Bube

» We work best in ministry when we are serving within our gifts and talents.

» "My fully exploited strengths are of far greater value to the kingdom than my marginally improved weaknesses." Andy Stanley

» Jesus is looking for normal people like you and me to tirelessly surrender ourselves to a higher calling.

Questions

» With regard to recruiting, how has competition and striving affected you?

» How have your "daddy/mommy issues" affected the way you view God?

» Why do you sometimes neglect Jesus' message of evangelism? How can you change this?

» How does being appointed to eternal life make you feel?

» At the end of your life, what is the one thing you wish to really have made a difference?

*value
people*

hen you read through the gospels, you will find that Jesus was not a popular household name among the religious leaders of His day. He repeatedly upset the church leaders with His teachings. He thwarted their meticulous rules and regulations. He challenged their rituals, which were birthing attitudes of hierarchy within the church. He lowered their haughty altars of religion and instead glorified humility and meekness. What I love about Jesus is that He never stirred up controversy for the sake of controversy, yet He was always making a commotion. His message and parables were constantly upsetting some and radically changing others. He stood for a love that extended its arms to all. Unfortunately, the religious leaders of the first century disapproved of how far and to whom Jesus extended His love.

In the first century, eating with somebody meant that you accepted or approved of him or her. So when Jesus ate with tax collectors, adulteresses, and others on the fringe of society, He was showing

His acceptance of them. This infuriated the religious leaders, as it tainted the image of holiness they so fervently sought. What kind of reputation was Jesus suggesting, they questioned, by surrounding Himself with those on the periphery of society?

To modernize the scenario, imagine the pastor of your church regularly dining out with the local drug dealer. Don't you think this might stir up some controversy? Some would rally the evangelistic nature of it, thinking it as revolutionary in nature. Others would express their obvious disapproval. If the pastor were questioned on the topic, suppose the pastor's defense was simply, "We're friends." The answer would be unsatisfactory to many. How could a pastor befriend someone so despicable, someone so low on the moral totem pole? If it is true, does the pastor also support the activities this man engages in? It would appear unorthodox and immoral to many onlookers.

Here was Jesus, who was claiming to be the Messiah, dining with the lowest members of society. To accentuate the offense, Jesus used the religious men's Scriptures to justify His actions, which unnerved the religious leaders. In self-defense, they constantly tried trapping Jesus in their questions as they searched for contradictions in His ministry.

In Luke, an expert of the law is inquiring Jesus about the way to inherit eternal life. His question lays the foundation for what eventually moves into the story of the good Samaritan.

In the Jewish faith there were two schools of thought often debated. All Jews agreed that loving God was the most important commandment, but there were discrepancies about the second most important command. The question was, is it more important to stay clean by following the Old Testament laws (such as eating kosher, keeping the Sabbath holy, etc.), or was it more important to love your neighbor as yourself? Discussions often arose about which commandments carried more weight than others. So in this situation, what the expert of the law was essentially asking was to which school of thought did Jesus align His theology? And what was Jesus' answer? Love. It's most important to love your neighbor. After Jesus takes His position, the expert probes further. "And who is my neighbor?"

Up to this point, the expert and Jesus have agreed. But the expert wants to know exactly how far this commandment extends. How wide and how deep does this neighborly love have to go?

The natural given answer would have been "Anyone who is a Jew is your neighbor." It would have been a clear-cut answer with a specific start and finish to the neighborly limits. It would have been a perfectly satisfactory Jewish answer. But as Jesus so characteristically does, He begins to tell a story, one that depicts a truth that is entirely unexpected and uncomfortable to its listeners. He begins to tell the radical story of the good Samaritan.

Suit Coats and Religious Folks

The story takes place on the side of a road. The route referred to as the Road of Blood was a curving, heavily trafficked road between Jerusalem and Jericho. Because of its wealthy travelers and winding landscape, the alcoves were popular spots for ambush and theft. So it is no surprise that Jesus' story begins with an anonymous man getting mugged and left to die on the Road of Blood. The next couple of characters introduced into the plot are a priest and a Levite. These men, both religious people, are most likely traveling home from the temple and happen to pass the scene of the crime. Although Jesus does not elaborate on their thoughts or intentions, He specifically says that the priest and the

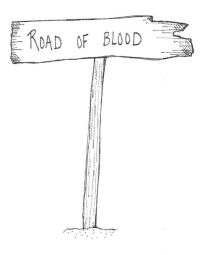

Levite saw the half-dead man and then proceeded to pass by on the other side of the road. It was not their most proud moment. I always assumed that these pompous religious dudes were self-conceited jerks, and that Jesus was teaching us that we should avoid being heartless like them. Eventually, the Samaritan man comes along, saves the day, and represents the nice guy we should all imitate. It is a cute story where Jesus teaches us to be the good guy and not the conceited jerk, right? Not quite. When we explore the various layers of this story, we find that Jesus was saying something much deeper and more significant.

There are many cultural pieces that we miss that make this story much richer than a tale about being kind. In the first century, the people who cared about religion and honoring God were consumed with following the Old Testament laws of clean and unclean. When a law was violated, the process of becoming clean was demanding. It required a trek to the temple, the sacrificing of a heifer until it was reduced to ashes, and a period of waiting at the temple for seven days. Not only would this have been a nuisance, but it also would have been disruptive to a family's income, wages, and livelihood. One of the laws of cleanliness forbade coming into contact with a dead body (Leviticus 21:11). Even if their shadow fell upon a dead body, they would become contaminated (Acts 5:15). Knowing about this specific law explains why the priest and Levite passed by on the opposite side of the road. If the man had, in fact, been dead, it would have been their religious obligation to pass by. There was too much at stake for them if they became unclean. Therefore, they did not attend to the body, dead or alive, because they dared not contaminate their shadow.

Considering the two passersby as religiously obedient by avoiding the fallen gentlemen is a twist that borders on bewildering. However, if we were in the same place, I wonder how we would respond. There was a morning when Pastor Bryan experienced a starkly similar scenario on his way to a presbyter's meeting. Walking from his house, wearing dress shirt and pants, he saw an elderly woman take a hard fall on the sidewalk. She hit the pavement with such force that he heard the thud. In that moment he had to make a quick decision. Helping the woman would inevitably mean his being late to his meeting, and his first thought was, "This is going to take awhile." But his second thought was, "There's no way I'm going to do this." The woman was disoriented, and her head was bleeding, but Pastor Bryan cared for her until she was back with her family.

He then jumped into the car and headed to meet with the other pastors in the district. With bloodstains on his shirtsleeve, his entire drive was penetrated with thoughts of the good Samaritan story. It was ridiculous to think for a second that I had a decision to make, he thought. Yet his religious responsibilities had threatened to interfere with his care for a person. How quickly we can become the Levite. The good Samaritan story is a bold one that causes us to peer into the looking glass, cringing but amazed that God bothers with us at all.

The Curious Protagonist

In stark contrast to the religious leaders, Jesus introduced the Samaritan man into the story. The animosity between Jews and Samaritans at the time was hefty, their history laced with hatred and prejudice. When Jesus positioned a Samaritan man as the protagonist of the story, He immediately instigated a controversy. It was like telling the story of the good atheist or the good racist. It is offensive, and for the audience to whom Jesus was addressing, it was most unfavorable to frame the Samaritan as the good guy. Yet the Samaritan man does what the religious leaders dared not do.

What Jesus did here was brave. He chose a person He knew was despised among the hearers of the story and elevated the Samaritan as the hero. Why did He do it?

Jesus wanted to make His answer to the question, "Who is my

neighbor?" painfully obvious. Not only was He showing us how to care for people, but He was also showing us who to care for and to what extent. A pastor from Rock Harbor, Mike Erre, shared the following in a sermon: "In this story, the expert of the law asks, 'Who is my neighbor?' and Jesus answers with 'Who is your enemy? …That man is your neighbor."[1] This powerful illustration teaches us that no one is exempt from the neighborly embrace. No one.

When Jesus finished the story, He asked the expert as to which one was the neighbor. The scholar answered, "The one who had mercy on him." He could not even utter the word Samaritan but instead uttered the word mercy. And so the story we thought was about being the nice guy is actually about putting away our pride, hatred, prejudice, and religious piousness and embracing a love for people that is so radical and countercultural that it could only be an example of the way Jesus valued people.

Q: Whose name do you struggle to say?

Prayer to Do Good

> Forgive me, most gracious Lord and Father, if this day I have done or said anything to increase the pain of the world. Pardon the unkind word, the impatient gesture, the hard and selfish deed, the failure to show sympathy and kindly help where I had the opportunity, but missed it; and enable me so to live that I may daily do something to lessen the tide of human sorrow and add to the sum of human happiness.
>
> —F. B. Meyer, England 1847-1929

---

1   Mike Erre, "Won't You Be My Neighbor," *ITunes* (audio blog), October 31, 2010, section goes here, https://itunes.apple.com/us/podcast/mariners-church-mission-viejo/id391234784.

How Do We Value People Like Jesus?

Acknowledge People

Long distance is the worst form of relationship in my opinion. It is hard work, and I'm terrible at it. I say this plainly, not proudly. My excuse is this: I aim to be fully present wherever I am. I shrug people off because I am investing into those surrounding me. "If I'm not near the ones I love, I love the ones I'm near" is a phrase I heard once and have adopted. Regardless of who truly matters the most, I would ignore phone calls and avoid messages for no reason other than I was busy. I was consumed by the events, social calendar, and personal well-being of my current setting. Hence, my long-distance relationships suffered.

This year, an out-of-state friend was growing frustrated from numerous failed attempts to contact me to see how I was doing. I had good intentions to call her back but never seemed to find the time. Finally, she wrote a long letter and sent it to me through the archaic postal system. Surprised, I found her letter in the mail and opened the envelope. Her scrawled words expressed her disappointment and hurt. "I know your life is busy," she wrote, "and I know you get caught up in where you are, but sometimes you make me feel like your time is more valuable than mine."

Her words were laced with truth. I realized that day that I had been mismanaging my relationships. I had been mismanaging people. By choosing when, how frequently, and to whom I would correspond, I had adopted the habit of prioritizing my time over everyone else's. At the root of the issue, I had befriended selfishness. I wondered, if I am treating people who I care about the most haphazardly, how am I treating everyone else? It was a frightening thought. I had allowed selfishness to creep into my relationships and dictate my actions.

I doubt I'm alone in this. Once or twice, you have probably been caught red-handed in the act of selfishness. In our self-absorbed culture, we are always being told to better ourselves, look out for number one, and do what we please when we so desire. It is natural and even socially acceptable to be selfish. We do so unknowingly, hardly realizing that we are harming those around us. Yet we all know better. We know that living selfishly is not the best way to live. If so, loneliness would be a joy. And we would despise words like community. Innately, we know that we exist in part to be available to others.

Although we are not to be doormats to everyone who demands our attention, it is important to understand that no one person is more valuable than another. Our time and needs are of no greater importance than the next person's. We will always struggle to make the right decision to help others if we are convinced that our time is more important than theirs.

Shifting the Focus Away from Me

We each place a high level of importance on our own lives. It's what comes naturally to us. We want to protect ourselves from hurt. We desire health, love, and success for our own good. We want to make a living, start a family, accumulate wealth, and live comfortably—all for the sake of our own happiness. On a daily basis, we meticulously care for our appearance and how others perceive us. We are selfish by nature. Even those in the depths of depression, who struggle with suicidal thoughts or battle sickness, are selfish. We could argue that those who have contempt for their own life surely must be exempt. However, I would argue that they, too, are consumed by their own pain and still put themselves first. Ironically, self-loathing is a form of self-love because it continues to place an obsession on self. At the stem of selfishness is a love of self. Yet Jesus challenges us to love every person with the same magnitude we choose to love ourselves.

The Samaritan teaches us that there are no exceptions to the rule. Our outpouring of love is not based on a system of deserving or undeserving. Once we grasp that loving everyone entails ...well, everyone, our task becomes incredibly difficult. It means that the dishonest friend, the aggravating coworker, the crazy family member, the cheating ex, the stranger seated next to you with the offensive stench are not exceptions. Each one is your neighbor. Each one is a person worthy of our pausing on the side of the road to assist and give of our time, resources, and, yes, even our love.

Recognizing a person's worth starts at a foundational level. It starts with seeing. Too often, we walk around like we are wearing blinders, passing by people who are desperate for human attention. We do not greet people when we pass them on sidewalks. We silently face elevator doors as we move from floor one to floor twenty. We hardly exchange a "how are you?" with the cashier in the grocery store. We treat each other like wallflowers. A smile exchanged in public is a rarity. Imagine if, for one day, everyone in the world walked around like we saw each other. Imagine how much we could brighten each other's paths.

In the good Samaritan story, all three passersby excelled in one area: the act of seeing the need. Jesus specifically tells us that the Levite and the priest both saw the injured man. Their eyes were open. There was a basic acknowledgment of another person in their path. However, the story goes askew with the inner workings of their minds. Instead of seeing the man's worth, they saw him as disposable. They looked at him through jaded human eyes instead of the lens of compassion. If they had given him a second glance, perhaps the story would have ended differently. Perhaps they would have seen him as a blessing rather than a burden.

Their Lives Tell a Story

When have you encountered someone who is harsh, rude, or just generally unlikeable? It probably happens frequently. In fact, you might be one of them! When you do, do you ever wonder what went wrong? Eventually, you get to know the person and find out that they had a rough past. Perhaps you learn they were abused or abandoned as a child. Maybe they dealt with an ugly divorce. Or you learned that they had recently been diagnosed with cancer. Essentially, you learn about that person and gain a deeper understanding of where they are coming from. You learn the fabric of their lives, which dictates their behavior, demeanor, and mannerisms. Hearing someone's story gives you grace to see that person with a new set of eyes.

In the book Weird, Pastor Craig Groeschel writes about an incident that changed his outlook on people. Craig was guest speaking at a church, and before the service began, a woman called the church office to ask for directions. Life had handed her some hard knocks, she explained on the phone, and she was finally resigning herself to "give church a try." Pulling into the church lot, she found a parking space for her beat-up car. She stomped out her cigarette and approached the  front doors, wearing clothes that revealed more skin than the apparel of most church attenders. The greeter at the door, a cranky old man named Virgil, quickly surveyed her attire and welcomed her with a stern lecture on her unsuitable appearance. The visitor stopped in her tracks, stared at Virgil for a couple moments, and walked right back to her car. I imagine a woman whose head hung in dismay, whose shoulders slumped, whose heart broke. It turns out the church had not offered her reprieve from the harshness of the rest of the world.

Although most of us would like to slap Virgil for his judgmental dismissal, if we were positioned at the front doors, I wonder what would have crossed our minds. Would we have wondered about her story? Would we have seen her as a person who needed the love of Jesus? Or would we too have surveyed her appearance and made quick judgments? Craig said,

> I realized that day that blessings come in a variety of shapes, colors, and sizes ...God's blessings, however, aren't always bigger, better, and beautiful. In fact, I truly believe that God gifts His chosen leaders with a very unusual blessing. You might even call it a weird blessing because most of the time we call it ...a burden. [2]

When we shift the way we see people who are in our way, are not like us, or bewilder us, it turns our burdens into blessings and our judgments into compassion. The truth about loving people the way Christ loved is a large one. We can't miss it, for it is of utmost importance.

One summer evening, a few friends of mine circled around a fire in the backyard. So as not to disturb the calm night, we spoke in quiet tones, discussing the small matters of our lives and started articulating our recent frustrations with the church and its people. After listening for a long time, my friend Steven, who had been quiet for a while, finally spoke up.

"I love the church and its imperfect people," he said thoughtfully. "I just think that too often we don't take Jesus' message of love seriously enough. I think we've convinced ourselves that tolerance is the same as love, but they are nothing alike." He said how tolerance means we "put up" with people but nothing in our heart stirs for them. We applaud ourselves for putting up with the unlikable person, but Jesus

---

2   Craig Groeschel, *Weird: Because Normal Isn't Working* (Grand Rapids, Mich: Zondervan, 2011).

never called us to tolerate people. "If we are called to love people," he said, "tolerance is not an option."

Q: We are called to love everyone as ourselves. Not just our family and close friends—everyone. How would we love differently if we truly grasped this truth?

Q: In what ways do you exchange love for tolerance? How does that difference come to light in the way you treat people who are different from you?

Have a Heart of Compassion

When the Samaritan first saw the beaten figure along the side of the road, he came over to him and "took pity on him." In Greek, pity is a very strong word that refers to the inner recesses of the stomach and bowels, encompassing the deep feelings evoked from within.[3] It describes what compassion feels like. Pastor Bryan likens compassion to "your hurt in my heart."

Ecclesiastes 4:9–10 explains, "Two are better than one, because they have a good return for their labor: If either of them falls down, one can help the other up. But pity anyone who falls and has no one to help them up." Understanding the correct usage of the word pity deepens the entire message. Pity is no longer a fleeting thought of sadness over someone's plight. Instead, it invites us to feel a deep sadness from within as if it were our own. It instructs us to take it personally when we see someone else's struggle.

We all want to be understood at a personal level. None of us yearn for unsympathetic understanding. If our dog died, we wouldn't want to hear, "Don't take it personally. It was only a dog." We would want someone who feels compassion for our loss and is personally stirred

---

3   Thayer and Smith. "Greek Lexicon Entry for Oiktirmos." "The KJV New Testament Greek Lexicon."

by the pain we feel, not because it is their own pain, but because it is a personal pain. We crave that kind of intimacy.

Jesus always met people at a deeply personal level. That is why people flocked to Him. He took his neighborly responsibility to heart and did not reserve it for an exclusive few. He did not divvy it up solely among family members, disciples, and close friends. Continuously, the wounds of people who crossed Jesus' path instantly and deeply moved Him. Encounters of mere happenstance turned into divine encounters when Jesus responded to people through compassion. From a well to a crowded street to a road to Damascus, Jesus revealed Himself to people who would normally have been judged and excused in an instant. Adulteress. Diseased. Murderer. Yet He learns their story, sees their need, and takes it personally. He pulls them in and accepts them. He eats with them and offers them eternal nourishment. Jesus sees people and then responds to them with massive compassion.

This was astounding to those who walked and talked with Him then, but the awesome news is that Jesus is still in the same business. Jesus still sees people. He sees us with our wounds, heartaches, and messiness and feels a guttural ache from within for us. As much as a heart can ache for another, Jesus hurts for us. And He is yearning to offer His healing compassion.

The rest of this chapter about loving people and valuing their personhood is futile if we do not apply it to ourselves. The sole instance in this book where selfishness will be presented in a positive light is here. Take advantage of it, and understand that the kind of love and sympathy described is meant, first and foremost, for you. Reflecting God's love is impossible until we launch ourselves onto the shores of its greatness. Romans 8:38 assures us, "Neither death nor life, neither angels nor demons, neither the present nor the future, nor any powers, neither height nor depth, nor anything else in all creation, will be able to separate us from the love of God that is in Christ Jesus our Lord" (NIV). There is no room within that promise for guesswork about the extent of God's immense love. I hope you fully grasp this truth. Because once you understand that God's deep love and compassion is for you, you are at a good starting place.

A Tattoo Artist and Church

We sat in a Subway for lunch. The smell of deli meat, hoagies, and sterilizers from the tattoo shop next door intermingled, creating an unpleasant aroma. Walking up for a refill of soda, my dad stood next to a burly guy whose brawny arms were covered in tattoos. I assumed he came from next door. They struck up conversation, and the guy followed him back to the table to join us for lunch.

Table talk livened as we chatted with this guy, Joe, who, it turns out, owned the adjoining tattoo shop. He talked for a majority of the time about his work and art. His prized tattoo was an inked portrait of his four-year-old daughter. The outline of her face was positioned proudly on his bulging bicep. After a half hour or so, the conversation shifted when Joe asked about my dad's profession. Joe's expression of inquiry turned to pure surprise when my dad told him he was a pastor. I suppose Joe was shocked that we would bother with him at all with his tattoos and rough language. He admitted that he had never been too fond of church. My dad explained how he helps start new churches and works with pastors. "Joe, if we were going to plant a church that you would go to, what would it look like?" Dad asked him.

I will never forget his answer. Joe said, "When I get home from work every day and walk through the door, my daughter runs up to me and gives me a big hug. She doesn't care about the way I look or how many tattoos or piercings I have. She doesn't care about those things. If I could find a church with that kind of acceptance, I would go there." A few minutes later, Joe gave us a tour of the tattoo shop, and we parted ways. But his words continued to disturb me. He never mentioned having a problem with religion or Jesus or the Bible. The reason Joe did not go to church was because he didn't feel accepted by the people there. If Jesus would have befriended Joe, why wouldn't the church?

I had compassion for Joe. I liked him and hoped that one day he would find a church that would accept him and his four-year-old daughter. A church that would love them into the kingdom, not in a clichéd way, but in a deeply personal sense out of love and genuine compassion. In 1 Peter 3:8–9, we are directed, "Be like-minded, be sympathetic, be compassionate and humble. Do not repay evil with evil or insult with insult. On the contrary, repay evil with blessing, because to this you were called so that you may inherit a blessing." When we replicate the greatness of Jesus' love, compassion grows hands and feet. Compassion obtains ears that will listen and soft words that will console. Compassion does not judge or condemn. Compassion looks like you and me, and love flows out into a wounded world.

Turning Compassion into Action

> It is in God that we find our neighbors and discover our responsibility to them. We might even say that only in God does our neighbor become a neighbor rather than an infringement upon our autonomy, and that only in and through God does service become possible.
>
> —Henri Nouwen [4]

---

4   Henri J. M. Nouwen, *The Living Reminder: Service and Prayer in Memory of Jesus Christ* (New York: Seabury Press, 1977)

The message is pretty clear up to this point. Every single solitary person on this earth is our neighbor. Our neighbors are everyone we see, and each one has a story. Everyone's story is worthy of compassion, and we are the means of compassion. John Townsend said, "People with skin on them are God's delivery system of His grace."[5] And grace, according to John, comes in all forms: comfort, acceptance, truth, understanding, empathy, and wisdom. Whatever form people need it, we have been called to deliver. As participants in the good Samaritan story, we have reached the area of tension. A burden can stay inside for only so long until it turns into action or inaction. How do you react to the burdens stirring within you? When you feel pity toward someone who is homeless, how do you respond? When you feel sorrow for someone who has lost his or her job, how do you react?

Once you feel burdened, there are two potential outcomes. The first is easy, as it requires nothing from you. It is the gradual death of your burden due to delay or inaction. Allowing the compassion to sit within you for so long that it is eventually forgotten. Inaction causes something that had the potential to grow to die instead. We allow this to occur when we do not put our compassion into action. As Christ-followers, it is clear that inaction is not the path we should take. God advocates for us to reveal what is in our hearts through our actions.

In Isaiah 58:6–8, God's chosen people are starting to get cranky. They complain heavenward because they have fasted, prayed, and visited the temple daily yet fail to see God's fruitfulness. It is because God is frustrated with His people for the inconsistency between their words and their actions. Although they were faithful in fasting, their actions toward one another were unkind and wicked. They "kept on fighting and quarreling" and "going through the motions of penance." To explain His desire for them, God states,

---

5   John Townsend, "Adventures in Relationship" (sermon, Mariners Church, Irvine, CA), http://mariners.aspireonemedia.com/.

This is the kind of fasting I want: Free those who are
wrongly imprisoned; lighten the burden of those who
work for you. Let the oppressed go free, and remove the
chains that bind people. Share your food with the hungry,
and give shelter to the homeless. Give clothes to those who
need them, and do not hide from relatives who need your
help. Then your salvation will come like the dawn, and
your wounds will quickly heal. (Isaiah 58:6–8 NLT)

A huge part of God's character is illuminated through these
commands. He is informing us that our good intentions don't impress
Him, nor does our empty religion. Instead, He wants us to care for
one another with fervency, and to remove any questions on our end,
He provides us with a list of specifics: share your food, give shelter,
provide clothes, and assist your family. We can appreciate that God
removes the guesswork for us.

Very simply, God desires that we put our love into tangible
form through action. Yes, this requires risk; it takes up our time and
soaks up our energies, but it undoubtedly is our only option if we are
surrendered to obeying God. C. S. Lewis writes, "I may repeat 'Do as
you would be done by' till I am black in the face, but I cannot really
carry it out till I love my neighbor as myself; and I cannot learn to love
my neighbor as myself till I learn to love God: and I cannot learn to
love God except by learning to obey Him."[6]

God is compassionate, and He will not strike us if we fail to act
on every impulse of compassion. Thankfully, He offers us grace in the
process. Yet He desires for us to grow into our love muscle because He
knows that it will also enhance our character and our faith. Our acting out
in compassion creates oneness with Him. Since Jesus sacrificed Himself
for us, how better can we relate to Him than through doing the same?

---

6   C. S. Lewis, *Mere Christianity: A Revised and Amplified Edition, with a New
     Introduction, of the Three Books, Broadcast Talks, Christian Behaviour, and
     Beyond Personality* (San Francisco: Harper San Francisco, 2001)

Turkey Dinner or a Wedding?

Todd is the kind of guy you want to be friends with. He is the children's pastor at Glad Tidings and would bend over backward for anyone—back bend, cartwheel, somersault, you name it. He is the guy who gets the job done. When we were raising money for water wells in Africa, I was in charge of constructing a display for the atrium. Our church's goal was to encourage each person to fill a water bottle with loose change and drop it off at the display I was supposed to create. Although I was the creative arts specialist at the time, my stress level was infringing on my creativity. Todd heard about it and said, "I'll see what I can do." Within hours, he had procured a twenty-foot-wide by ten-foot-high chain link fence, spelled out the word hope using water bottles, and set it up in the atrium. It was an impressive construction. That's the kind of guy Todd is.

A couple of years ago, Todd was invited to a wedding at the church on a Saturday. For anyone who works at a church, if your services are on Sunday, your Sabbath is not also Sunday. Sundays are hectic filled with questions, directing, and all forms of ministry—the summation of a week's worth of preparation. For most staff members who work at the church, Saturdays are a better fit for a day of rest. But this Saturday was an exception since there was a wedding.

It was a brisk fall day, and Thanksgiving was right around the

corner. Guests filed through the front doors, and the energy hinted that the ceremony was about to begin. Todd entered the church and noticed a family lingering by the side doors, looking confused. His first instinct was to keep walking so he wouldn't be late to the ceremony. But his second instinct and stronger impulse directed him to the doors to investigate. The family explained that they had heard about the church's turkey collection for Thanksgiving dinners. They said they didn't attend Glad Tidings, but they had a carload of turkeys to drop off and didn't know where to take them.

He had a decision to make. Todd stood at the side doors of the church on his day off in his wedding outfit. He could ask the family to return during church hours, give them the number of the person in charge, or he could assist them.

Todd missed the wedding that day. He also worked a little on a Saturday. But Todd was able to talk to a family about the church and help them unload all their turkeys. Todd chose to put his love for people—people he didn't know and who turned up at an inconvenient time—before himself. I don't know if I would have done what Todd did that day. I would like to think I would. I know that Todd did what Jesus would've done if He had been at the church that Saturday. I think it makes God proud of us when we care for His own in such tangible ways, especially when it requires a hard decision, and we make the right one.

Bad Outcomes

Sometimes our compassion is met with gratitude, but that's not always the case. Sometimes helping people is as rewarding as watching paint dry. This was one of those times.

It was late, and I was starving. I pulled into the Jack in the Box parking lot and entered the drive-thru lane. As I was looking over the menu options, in my peripheral vision, I spotted a homeless woman sitting on the sidewalk in front of the fast-food joint. Assuming she was hungry, I thought it would be a kind gesture to buy her a sandwich, so I ordered myself a cheeseburger and purchased a second one for her. It seemed like a good idea at the time, but when I pulled up in front of her to deliver the bag, I started to second-guess my decision, feeling uncomfortable and awkward. Saying a quiet prayer, I approached the woman, whose gray hair was sticking out all directions beneath her hat. Her scent hit me like a wall, and I wondered when she had last showered. Timidly, I said, "I thought you might be hungry, so I got you something." I offered her the bag. She didn't reach for it but nodded toward it. "What's in it?" she barked. I told her it was a cheeseburger, and she shook her head in disgust. I was confounded and managed a fumbled apology as I turned to go. "Leave it," she said. I gave her the bag and turned back to my car.

In hindsight, I should have said more, but in that moment, I was fearful and caught off guard. Regardless, what I realized that night is that when it comes to helping people, there won't always be a fixed reaction or response. If we are helping people for "feel good" purposes, most likely we are setting ourselves up for disappointment. Our actions will not always elicit our desired responses. In the story of the good Samaritan, we never know what happens when the wounded man awakens at the inn. Perhaps he was a Jew and was horrified that a Samaritan had the audacity to help him. What if the man harbored more animosity for the Samaritan than for the robbers? We don't know how the story ends, but Jesus does not make it a matter of importance. What was important were the actions through which he was helped and the attitude beneath them, not how the man responded.

There will be times when we'll want to fix someone who refuses to be fixed. There will be times when we'll go out of our way to assist someone and never receive proper thanks. There will be times when we'll be unacknowledged, misunderstood, misjudged, or ignored in our service to others. And this is what we are signing up for, with joy! Although lack of appreciation can be disheartening, it realigns the motives behind our actions. It reminds us that our actions are done as a service to God aimed toward people, not to people aimed toward praise for ourselves.

We can never know the eternal impact we have on people. A thankless task might be received by a person who shows no outward response but who was deeply impacted within. Although there is a real possibility that I annoyed the homeless lady by ordering her least favorite food item from the menu, there is the slight chance that she felt cared for if even for a fleeting moment. Maybe she appreciated that a young girl noticed her and wondered about her need. Maybe I gave her a small glimpse of God's love. I am not trying to appease myself with optimism, but I am suggesting that we will never know how much our actions impact others. There is no way to measure the tracings of love, but that does not underestimate the greatness of its existence.

Shane Claiborne, author of The Irresistible Revolution, wrote about his time spent working in Calcutta in the leper colony. "Even though I touched them, they still went home lepers at the end of the day."[7] Shane learned that serving was never about the end result; it was about something much more significant: love.

> What had lasting significance were not the miracles themselves but Jesus' love. Jesus raised his friend Lazarus from the dead, and a few years later, Lazarus died again. Jesus healed the sick, but they eventually caught some other disease. He fed the thousands, and the next day they were hungry again. But we remember his love. It wasn't that Jesus healed a leper but that he touched a leper, because no one touched lepers.[8]

Shadow

In the classic tale of Peter Pan, originally written by playwright J. M.

---

7   Shane Claiborne, *The Irresistible Revolution: Living as an Ordinary Radical* (Grand Rapids, MI: Zondervan, 2006).

8   Shane Claiborne, *The Irresistible Revolution: Living as an Ordinary Radical* (Grand Rapids, MI: Zondervan, 2006).

Barrie, Peter characterizes a young boy whose mischief and ignorance are symptoms of his rebellion against adulthood. Peter is an endearing scoundrel, introduced into the first act through the whimsical pursuit of his shadow, which loosed itself from his person. The stage directions describe the shadow as "a flimsy thing …yet it has human shape," insinuating that although it is an object, it inhabits the stage as tangibly as the other characters in the plot. In fact, the shadow guides the rising action of the play, keeping Peter in pursuit of its whereabouts. When Wendy finds Peter discouraged by his futile chase, she asks him if he was crying because he couldn't find his mother. "I wasn't crying about mothers," he said rather indignantly. "I was crying because I can't get my shadow to stick on. Besides, I wasn't crying." Although he denies his emotion, he admits that his shadow is problematic. This flimsy thing, which we normally associate as lifeless, was rebelling against Peter.[9]

A shadow, in the context of which we are familiar, is the image projected from a blocked light source. But throughout art, literature, and film, shadows conjure more abstract associations, such as fear, sadness, ignorance, guilt, and sin. A shadow is the most vivid representation of light trumping dark and the opposite. This interplay of light and darkness is constant inspiration for artists depicting mankind's inner turmoil. Shadows are surmised from a psychological perspective as

light trumps dark.

---

9   J. M. Barrie and Nora S. Unwin, *Peter Pan* (New York: Charles Scribner's Sons, 1950).

well. Psychologist Carl Jung describes a shadow as "the 'negative' side of the personality, the sum of all those unpleasant qualities we like to hide, together with the insufficiently developed functions and the contents of the personal unconscious."[10] B. Wharton described the shadow as a combination of what is not known and what is not liked. All of these connotations suggest, and I suppose Peter would agree, that although our shadow is our nearest companion, it is not necessarily our warmest one. Our shadow represents the part of us that went crooked. It is the villainous side of our intentions that displays darkness, and although it is a mere reflection, every once in a while, it takes the reigns and wreaks havoc. Our shadow becomes our rogue leader.

Why am I making such a fuss about the shadow, about that thing that is flimsy enough to seem inconsequential but substantial enough to take shape and manifest itself through our activities? Because when two religious people who were savvy enough to know the difference between right and wrong, holy and unholy, they allowed their shadows to dictate the end of the story. You got it—the priest and the Levite were steered by the promptings of their shadows. I do not aim to villainize these two passersby despite my continual praise of the Samaritan and criticism of these guys. As mentioned previously, Jewish moral law specified that if even their shadow were tainted, they would become unclean. There was no way for the priest or Levite to evaluate if the wounded man was dead or alive, Samaritan or Jew, without getting close enough to chance the contamination of their shadow.

The shadow brings us insights because it interplays with the question presented on the road to Jericho, "Will you serve your neighbor?" It is the same question that we are asked on a daily, sometimes hourly, basis. "Will you serve your family member?"

---

10   C. G. Jung and Mrs Beatrice Moses Hinkle, *Psychology of the Unconscious; a Study of the Transformations and Symbolisms of the Libido, a Contribution to the History of the Evolution of Thought,* (New York: Moffat, Yard and, 1916), pg. 10.

"Will you serve your coworker?" "Will you serve a stranger?" And often what stands in the way between responding with a hearty yes or a heavy no is a dark shadow clouding our view of the need and justifying our reasons for passing by.

Shadows Come in All Disguises

We are about to explore the various forms of the shadow that evidence themselves within our lives. In spite of their distinctions, each one is destructive to altruism and catastrophic to the purposes of selfless love. Although they are worthy excuses, they prevent us from fulfilling what God claimed to be the first and second most important commands: loving God and loving others. Charles Spurgeon said, "I never knew a man refuse to help the poor who failed to give at least one admirable excuse!"[11] There are probably more, but here is a list of six common shadows that prevent us from reaching out to others and the mentalities to combat each one.

(I suggest that you don't skip over any, assuming it doesn't pertain to you. Often our shadows are hidden from us, so read each one with an open mind.)

1. Busyness

Busy schedules cast a shadow on our service. All of us have pulled out these excuse at some time or another: "I was in a hurry," "I wanted to get home," or even "I would have been late to such-and-such church function!" Our busyness that consumes us begs the question, Are we in charge of our schedules or are they in charge of us? If you ever look at your calendar and break out in a mild case of hives, you might want to pay attention to this one.

Our lives are hectic. Our schedules pile a mile high, and we say it

---

11 C. H. Spurgeon and Charles T. Cook, *C.H. Spurgeon's Sermons on the Parables* (Grand Rapids, MI: Zondervan, 1958).

is only for a season, but do we ever see it ending? If we are not making time for people, even in the inconvenient, unplanned circumstances, we need to realign our priorities. One way of knowing a person's priorities is by looking at how he or she distributes his or her time. If your excuse for neglecting service is busyness or lack of time, you might want to ask God if He wants you to release some of your current commitments. Remember that you cannot put new things on your plate without inevitably pushing other things off. If God is asking us to fit serving others onto our plate, which He unquestionably is, what is He asking us to take off our plate?

Looking back on several busy seasons of my life—times when I was barely keeping my head above the water—shifting my focus to others was impossible. I could hardly maintain my own well-being. God does not desire for us to take on so many things at an arbitrary pace. He challenges us to hone in on a few areas and do them with great care. As A. W. Tozer said, "When you kill time, remember that it has no resurrection." [12]

Nobody was busier than Jesus, but He allowed for His ministry to be based on interruptions. Why? Because He made time for people. Do not allow busyness to block the opportunities to give grace to those in need around you.

2. Reputation

No one thinks, "Well I don't help others because it will ruin my reputation." However, consider the reverse. Does it better your reputation and increase your likeability to be the helpful one? Those whose shadow is their reputation are the sort of people who choose when they want to be neighborly on a case-by-case basis. They are the ones who are constantly concerned about how their actions will be perceived by others. The person concerned with their reputation

---

12   Craig Groeschel, *Weird: Because Normal Isn't Working* (Grand Rapids, Mich: Zondervan, 2011).

says, "I will help my neighbor if the people watching me approve" or "I will help my neighbor if it benefits me."

The only way to reconcile this is to look to Jesus. The truth is that following Jesus can be hopelessly uncool, especially when it comes to whom you are keeping company. As I mentioned earlier, Jesus made a lot of people angry with the kind of people he hung around. Nowadays, we admire how Jesus hung out with those on the fringe of society because it was rebellious, which is hip. But in the first century, it was not so. Jesus received a lot of frowns, specifically from the ones who cared about their reputation.

We can be thankful that Jesus did not care about reputation. Jesus did not say to the leper, "Sorry, man, but you're an outcast. I can't be seen around you. My PR guy wouldn't like that." He did not say to Zacchaeus, "Thanks for the dinner offer, but you're a tax collector. That could destroy my social status." If Jesus had cared about His reputation, the gospel would have turned out very differently. But Jesus knew He was not leading a trendy social club, nor was He consumed by image. He befriended those who were ignored and scorned by society. Befriending the least of these may maim your reputation, but it will return your heart to its rightful state. Paul tells us in Philippians 2:3 to "do nothing out of selfish ambition or vain conceit, but in humility consider others better than yourselves" (NIV).

If you hesitate to help the "losers" of society—those who dress poorly, smell badly, have addictions, live on the streets, are diagnosed with AIDS, or have a low economic status—perhaps you should ask Jesus to help you care less about your reputation.

3. Prejudice and Preconceived Notions

There are similarities between prejudice and reputation, as both are dictated by the receivers of our kind acts. The primary difference is that reputation is outer-based and prejudice is inner-based. Reputation shifts depending on environment and audience, but prejudice is a stubborn fixed position of the heart that colors our actions. It is a subtle hatred or judgment that dictates the way we interact with the world.

Do not assume you are exempt from this one. I would dare to say that every person, resulting from personal experience or generalized assumption, harbors prejudices that interact with their worldview, knocking their compassion meter off-kilter. Although you might not have grudges against a particular race or religion, perhaps you espouse a mind-set of "They get what they deserve," which is its own form of prejudice.

Countless times I've heard people (Christians included) say of the homeless, "Why should I help them if they are too lazy to get a job?" or "I don't want to give them money because they'll probably spend it on drugs or alcohol." None of these statements reflect sympathy or love.

One of my college professors bluntly challenged us to always give to the homeless. He said, "We are not responsible for what they do with the money. That's none of our business. Our responsibility is what God directed us to do—which is to give." He compared it to the way we were entrusted with a higher education without the stipulation that we wouldn't abuse it. Education was given to us with the hopes of betterment but not a guarantee of it. It is the same concerning how we interact with the pregnant teenager, the homosexual, the young, the old, the criminal, and the atheist. Not with a pompous attitude, but with one of compassion that is bestowed with the hopes of betterment.

People who struggle with prejudices or preconceived notions believe that certain people are undeserving of love, grace, or service, but in actuality, none of us deserve love, grace, or service. If you struggle in this area, pray that God will help you to believe the best about people, and reach out in love to those who look nothing like us, talk nothing like us, and act nothing like us.

4. Fear and Insecurities

Some people are stirred by compassion, but the shadow that separates them from action is fear and insecurity. Fear can paralyze us from rising to the occasion. Addressing a need like when I gave the sandwich to the woman at the fast-food restaurant required courage on my part. It is not easy to act on impulses of compassion. It can be even more intimidating reaching out to people we know, for it opens the doors wider to rejection.

We all deal with the feelings of "not enough." If you are placed in someone's life and your heart is stirring with compassion for him or her, you are enough. We should not imagine that we must become the "right" person with the perfect words and the proper knowledge in order to be an asset to anybody. Sometimes we simply need to be the person who happens to be available. If you are waiting until fear flees, you will live your life waiting, shirking your calling, and becoming insignificant to the people who need you.

Author and speaker Carol Kent travels and shares about her son, who murdered a man and was given a lifelong sentence in jail. In an interview, she talked about a random interaction in the bathroom of a jail.

> Last Christmas, I was visiting Jason at the prison …I was sitting in one of the stalls in the ladies' room, and I heard a woman come in. She was sobbing and cussing. She said, "I hate this place, I hate these people, I think I'm having a nervous breakdown!" The old professional side of me would have gone to her and quoted my best five verses about suffering. I would have prayed for her, patted her on the back, and told her "I am so sorry." But the new me stepped out and put my arms around her and wept with her. I told her, "I know what this feels like, I'm a mom too; it hurts so much." She wasn't ready for my verses; she wasn't ready for a prayer; she just needed to know

that another mother cared. I'm learning so much—that God uses broken people to minister to broken people. The old me was what some would have called a professional, a highly educated woman with a thriving ministry, but the new me is a crushed me, a speaker who identifies with the pain of people. My husband and I have learned that pain is pain is pain is pain. For one person, it's that their husband left. For another, their child was born with a disability, or for still another, a financial disaster has altered their life. But pain is pain.[13]

Carol's story is brimming with raw authenticity, which is what people crave most. Not coined compassion or professional charity. Step out, even when you feel inadequate. If a need seems too big or a person too intimidating, it could be that God challenging you to see if you are up for it. It's when we are most fearful that we have the greatest opportunity for personal growth. The question is not "succeed or fail" when dealing with people. The question is "Will you influence others for the sake of the kingdom or will you remain paralyzed by your fear?"

5. Laziness

The shadow of laziness is perhaps the most common reason that we fail to turn our compassion into action. It is more a numbing than conscious reasoning. We do not seize the initial opportunity to reach out in love because it involves too much. It sucks up our time, resources, and efforts, and we are not feeling up to it. Phrases like "I don't feel like it," "I am too tired," "It is too difficult," or "I'll put it off until tomorrow" all surface in the name of laziness.

A common symptom of sickness is slothfulness. Who feels up to

---

13   "Interview with Carol Kent," interview by Carol Kent, Christianbook.com, section goes here, accessed July 22, 2013, http://www.christianbook.com/ Christian/Books/cms_content?page=855611&segment=1.

doing anything when they are sick? Awhile ago, a high fever kept me under the covers with a box of tissues. Throughout the week, I was asleep more than I was awake. One morning, at the cusp of my sickness, I read a devotional titled "Readiness" by Oswald Chambers. He wrote, "When God speaks, many of us are like people in a fog, and we give no answer."[14] It explained how we should be a ready people—ready to jump to action when God provides opportunity. I lay there reading—achy, weary, tired, and completely depleted of energy. To be honest, annoyance crept over me, and instead of being prompted to "get ready," I was irritated at this unrelenting call to action.

The truth is, many times we do move about like people in a fog, lacking answers. We are not ready because we keep pushing it off. We have separated our emotions from our behavior and have stopped showing up in our own lives.

Sometimes the hardest place to be is present in the moment and ready to take action. It requires so much consistent effort, but we are all being beckoned to a life defined by alive and alert spirits. We are called to be life embracers, not slothful sleepers. Paul writes in his letter to Ephesus, "Wake up, sleeper, rise from the dead, and Christ will shine on you. Be very careful, then, how you live—not as unwise but as wise, making the most of every opportunity, because the days are evil."[15] When Paul says that the days are evil, he is saying that time is working against us. We cannot afford to put off what is most important today in the name of laziness. Instead, we must learn to be intentional about action, and push aside our tendencies toward inaction and dulled senses.

Of the sin of laziness, each one of us is guilty. We can offer up this prayer and begin anew today. "Forgive me for letting love die when

---

14   Oswald Chambers and James Reimann, *My Utmost for His Highest: Selections for Every Day* (Grand Rapids, MI: Discovery House Publishers, 1995).

15   Ephesians 5:14

it demands action in order to live. Forgive me for not caring enough to mourn its death."[16]

6. Lack of Ownership

This last shadow is when we assign responsibility to someone else. We naively assume that someone else will be the hero, making us exempt. The priest and Levite might have reasoned, "There will be plenty of people traveling on this road. I'm sure someone else will help him," and walked away with their worries put to ease. How many times have you passed a break down on the side of the highway and wondered if you should assist but assume that someone else will take care of it?

By failing to take ownership of the needs around us, we miss the driving message of the good Samaritan story. When we see a need, it becomes our own. Our religion is empty if it does not compel us to reach out to those who are hurting who cross our path. What is impressive about the Samaritan is how he took his job seriously. He did not try to pass the baton to the next person. He poured oil and wine on the wounded man, the word pour insinuating lavish generosity. He didn't try to skirt the costs at the inn, which cost him two days wages. He returned the next day to check up on the man. When he decided to help, he took the burden on himself as though it were his own kin. He stood in the gap.

There is a beautiful depiction for us in Exodus about owning each other's concerns. War is raging between the Israelites and the Amalekites. Joshua is fighting in battle while Moses, the leader of the Israelites, climbs to the top of the hill with Aaron and Hur. Moses lifts the staff of God into the air, and whenever the staff is raised, the Israelites are winning, but whenever Moses lowers his arms, they are

---

16 Bill Dogterom, "Lenten Prayers - Sloth," *Something to Think About* (web log), March 31, 2011, Lenten Prayers, http://bdogterom.blogspot.com/2011_03_01_archive.html.

losing. As you can imagine, Moses' arms grow tired, and it is then that we see this wonderful display of ownership materialize. "When Moses' hands grew tired, they took a stone and put it under him and he sat on it. Aaron and Hur held his hands up—one on one side, one on the other—so that his hands remained steady till sunset. So Joshua overcame the Amalekite army with the sword" (Exodus 17:12–13 NIV). This story evokes such a clear image of how we are supposed to care for one another. I picture Moses, this strong leader, perhaps looking somewhat like Charlton Heston, and he is in the struggle, his muscles probably shaking from exhaustion. He is tired, weak, and scared of failure like so many of us. But his friends position themselves on both sides of him and hold his arms steady until the battle is won. They take complete ownership over their friend's struggle and stay committed until the task is complete.

When you face the temptation to pass the baton to the next person, I encourage you to stay in the race and be the one who will raise up someone's arms.

Turn Your Shadow into Light

"Maybe the only thing each of us can see is our own shadow." Carl Jung called this his shadow work. He said we never see others. Instead, we see only aspects of ourselves that fall over them. Shadows. Projections. Our associations. The same way old painters would sit in a tiny dark room and trace the image of what stood outside a tiny window in the bright sunlight. The camera obscura. Or as Chuck Palahniuk states, "Not the exact image, but everything reversed or upside down." [17]

A shadow can only exist when both light and darkness are present. Once we eliminate the shadow that prevents us from stepping into the adventure of service, we can be sources of light that illuminate God's love.

17　Chuck Palahniuk, *Diary: A Novel* (New York: Doubleday, 2003).

Once we start to see everyone as our neighbor, it can become incredibly overwhelming, for we will see a need everywhere we look. But we should be thankful for our heartsickness for other people because it is a sure sign that we are becoming more like Christ. We are not called to be rescuers, but we are called to be servants.

Simple Ways to be Neighborly:

1. Offer encouragement. Write a note to tell someone what he or she means to you. Offer comfort, praise, and support, and search for opportunities to encourage others.
2. Prayer. Pray and fast for others. Doing so calls on God on their behalf and helps us see people the way God sees them. It is really hard to harbor ill feelings for someone who you pray for. Prayer changes the way we see people.
3. Say, "Thanks." Pastor Bryan consistently encourages the staff members at GT to intentionally say "thank you" to someone they serve with each week. Appreciating someone through gratitude is a powerful way to express that you value them.
4. "Make friends for Jesus." —Bill Dogterom[18]

Chapter Summary

» Jesus stood for a love that extended its arms to all.
» Jesus' story of the good Samaritan provokes us to reconsider our definition of who our neighbor is.
» Jesus never called us to tolerate people; He calls us to love people.
» It is impossible to reflect God's love without first having launched ourselves onto the shores of its greatness.

---

18 Bill Dogterom, "VUSC Baccalaureate Address" (speech, Class of 2010 Baccalaureate Address, St. Andrew's Presbyterian Church, Costa Mesa, CA).

» When we replicate the greatness of Jesus' love, compassion grows hands and feet.

» When we act out in compassion, it creates a oneness with Jesus. Since Jesus sacrificed Himself for us, how better can we relate to Him than through doing the same?

» Our actions are done as a service to God aimed toward people; not to people aimed toward praise of ourselves.

» If we are not making time for people, even in the inconvenient, unplanned circumstances, we need to realign our priorities.

» There are six shadows that prevent us from reaching out to others: busyness, reputation, prejudice and preconceived notions, fear and insecurities, laziness, and lack of ownership.

» If you are placed in someone's life and your heart is stirring with compassion for them, you are enough.

» It's when we are most fearful that we have the greatest opportunity for personal growth.

Questions

» Whose name do you struggle to say?

» Do you need to ask God to help you believe the best about people?

» Do you need to ask God to help you reach out to people who look nothing like you?

» When am I most tempted to give into laziness?

» Who are the three people in your life right now whom you need to value at a higher level?

experience growth

A Mountain Respite

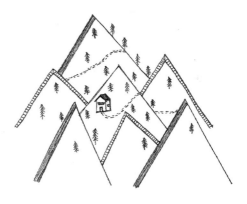

With a steady inhale, I allowed the alpine-infused air to fill my lungs and then reversed it. Its remnants appeared quickly and then vaporized into the frosty night. The tall trunks stood guard around the lodge as its branches waved a greeting. Night covered us, and the stars must have belonged to the mountains, as they were brighter and more spirited than usual. I found the key hidden beneath the carpet as promised, and let myself in. After distributing my bags and raiding the refrigerator for something satisfactory (cookie dough), I situated myself before the warm fire. This place was to be my hideaway and oasis for the next twenty-four hours. And with the assurance of solitude and complete unreachability, I drifted into sleep.

The next day, I hiked the worn mountain path in and out of prayer as I explored the rim of the forest. Back inside, with a brimming library, a music room, and a few unexpected inches of snow outside, the lodge provided the necessary space for me to detoxify. I questioned how I ended up here as I started to mentally review the past semester and a half. I was two hours removed from my college campus and two short steps away from a mental breakdown. The past months had been rough. I was a junior living in the freshmen dorm working for Residence Life. In other words, I was friend, counselor, and rule enforcer for forty energetic girls living away from home for the first time. Additionally, I worked a part-time job, carried a full course load, and kept a full social calendar. After a blurred, fast-paced semester, my frenzied schedule began to manifest itself through panic attacks and anxiety. And at that point, everything drastically slowed without my permission.

Counseling gradually helped ease me back into a livable normalcy, but I still felt very delicate. This mountain respite was a place for my thoughts and a time to talk with God. So I began to analyze how I ended up here, how I had become so fragile. How did an accumulation of good things lead me to such a bad emotional state?

This lodge set into the California mountain range was a place where people went for a spiritual retreat. It was for ministry leaders and pastors to hide away and reenergize their tired souls. A guest book sitting on the coffee table was filled with personal notes from previous inhabitants. As I began to read through their scripted thoughts, I noticed a repeated theme. These church-going, service-oriented, heavily invested ministry leaders came here fatigued, broken, and burned out. And they came here to mend. Like me, they must have reached some breaking point, which led them up this mountain. Here they prioritized their deeper spiritual needs over their usual tangible needs.

But why does this happen? When do genuinely good acts of service cross the line into the realm of burnout, anxiety, depression, and fatigue? When did the joys of serving become a task list of chores? And how do we recover?

Something reassuring about following Jesus is that the Bible reveals that He genuinely cares about our well-being. Although our faith is tested and our strength is tried, He wants to protect us from destruction. He befriends us, and His presence restores us to wholeness. Sometimes He simply desires to spend time with us, without our feeling like we have to perform.

There is an intimate story in the Bible that clearly depicts this. It does not take place in the streets of Jerusalem, in a marble temple, a dark garden, or a fishermen's boat. It is more personal than all of those places. It takes places in a living room. It is the story about Jesus and two sisters, Mary and Martha.

Invited into the Living Room

If Luke 10 is a chapter championing service, the Mary and Martha story is the final statement, the closing thought we are left to dwell on as we walk away from the idea of serving. And although the story provides a layer of finality to the message of service, it does so in a unique manner. First, Luke 10 depicts a larger-than-life recruitment of volunteers. Next, we hear a scandalous tale about a Samaritan man. But finally, within the concluding section of the chapter, everything slows down. Normalcy settles upon the scenery. We enter the living quarters of a small home in Bethany, where Jesus temporarily finds rest. Even the setting of the story, a home of two sisters, immediately welcomes us. It's not a large recruitment, a desperate harvest, or a mugging. It is a relatable story about a gathering inside a living room. Through this simplicity, we are invited to come into the private space where Jesus is staying, breathe deeply, watch, and listen.

On this particular occasion, the household has the demeanor

of a holiday party or a friendly gathering with the rush of last-minute preparations escalated by the arrival of guests. There was the scurrying, the straightening, and the last-minute sweeping as people begin to enter. The smell of baking bread wafts from the kitchen and saturates the other quarters of the house. The bedding has been washed and readied, and every inch of the house has been scrubbed, shined, and tidied. At least, that is what I imagine from a hostess like Martha. But what adds a unique dimension to this story is that instead of one hostess, we have two. And they are sisters.

From what can be estimated in the Gospels, Mary and Martha are related but differ considerably in personality. If given a first-century Myers-Briggs Personality Inventory, the results would have conveyed polar opposite results for these two women. One an extrovert; the other an introvert. One a feeler; the other a thinker. One neat; the other messy. And as with most sisters, drama unravels as opposing personalities lead to clashing opinions until Jesus answers on the subject.

In my family, I am the older of two girls, and if I were to guess, I would counter that Martha was also the oldest sister. She seems to take the reins in this story, starting with the initial invite she extends to Jesus and his entourage. Yet her actions spiral downhill under the commotion of the guests' arrival. As the guests begin to stream through the door, Martha is working feverishly on the last-minute arrangements. Meanwhile, her sister "sat at the Lord's feet listening to what he said. But Martha was distracted by all the preparations that had to be made" (Luke 10:40). What Martha says next is a classic "foot in the mouth" moment. But before shuddering at Martha's infamous two lines of dialogue, let's evaluate the preamble of what is going on internally for Martha.

The Infamous Discourse

Originally, when Martha mentally configured the party preparations, she assumed there would be four hands to pull the details together, hers and Mary's. But as soon as Jesus, the guest of honor, arrives, her sister disappears. With her sister's abandonment, Martha's stress mounts. Her worry grows. Her stride rushes. Becoming frantic as more people enter her home, Martha feels alone in her duties. She is in over her head. Ken Gire describes Martha's thought process in the kitchen:

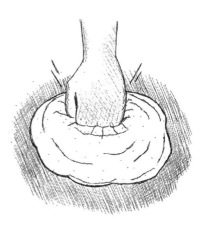

I can't believe Mary isn't in here helping, she thinks. Martha pushes a fist into the dough. She should be in here. Another fist into the dough. We could get this done in half the time. She pulls and mashes, pulls and mashes. You know, I'd like to hear what he has to say, too, but somebody's got to fix dinner. Martha reaches for some flour and flings it on the lump. They could at least come in here while they talk. She works the flour into the expanding loaf. I can't believe he just lets her sit there. Another fist into the dough. Here I am in the kitchen, sweating, working my fingers to the bone ... doesn't He care?[19]

And poking her head from the kitchen into the living room, there sits Mary, gazing up at Jesus. Perfectly contented. Without a worry in the world. And Martha reaches her breaking point.

Hearing this story as a kid, Martha annoyed me. Uptight and bossy, she seemed generally unlikeable. Although good intentioned, Martha creates a bad rep for herself in this brief account. But now as

19   Ken Gire, *Intimate Moments with the Savior: Learning to Love* (Grand Rapids, MI: Daybreak Books, 1989).

I reevaluate the relational and environmental dynamics as an adult, I see Martha's side. I understand her frustrations, and I even hear myself in her ensuing discourse, "Lord, don't you care that my sister has left me to do the work by myself? Tell her to help me!"

These honest frustrations reveal the misgivings of her heart. The first utterance being "Lord, don't you care?" Have you ever directed this question toward God? I have on multiple occasions. Martha feels abandoned, alone. She is overextended in her service. It is a classic story of someone who is burnt out from serving too much, for too long, by herself. Anyone who has been involved in ministry can relate to this at one point or another. And so when she asks, "Lord, don't you care?" her underlying message is "Hello! I am doing this for you, Lord, and You still don't care."

Next, she bosses around Jesus with the command "Tell her to help me." This is a wince-worthy comment. Whether Martha's tone was whiny, stern, or tearful, we can't distinguish from the text, but we can assume it was spoken with severity. In true type-A fashion, she is rattling off an order, certain to settle the matter and regain control, even if it means instructing the Messiah. And ashamedly, I can relate to Martha, yet again. Her rhetoric expresses the prayer many of us say silently when we give God an order under the guise of a prayer. We shoot our commands heavenward, certain we know what is best, even if He doesn't. Oftentimes, our prayers become the Martha cries of the "don't you care's" and the "do this" or "do that," especially when we are frazzled, exhausted, or depleted by our efforts of service.

According to the rules of serving, Martha seems to have done everything correctly. She was recruited and enlisted to service. Her attention to detail embraced excellence. She valued people by generously welcoming them into her home. But now, Jesus wants her to experience growth. Jesus wants to teach her what is better. And so He addresses her, not with a lecture or a mini-sermon, but as a friend. He looks at her with smiling, sympathetic eyes and meets her in her bedraggled state. "Martha, Martha ..." [20]The language sounds endearing, similar to when he spoke to Peter with "Simon, Simon, Satan has asked to sift you as wheat. But I have prayed for you, Simon, that your faith may not fail."[21] Or when he confronted Saul on the Damascus road, "Saul, Saul, why do you persecute me?"[22]

Perhaps Martha was softened solely from hearing Jesus speak her name. Jesus does this often. He meets us in our disasters and calls out our name to remind us of His presence and provision. Once Jesus has her attention, He says, "You are worried and upset about many things, but only one thing is needed. Mary has chosen what is better, and it will not be taken away from her" (Luke 10:42).

Martha points to her sister in accusation. Jesus points to Mary in illustration. And through it, Luke's final notation on service does not wrap up with a list of to-do's or additional tips, rules, and regulations. Instead, Jesus invites us to spend time with Him. It is so uncomplicated. So beautiful. And I think it's what Jesus wants to show us all along. It's what serving has always been about.

Like Martha, we complicate matters. Yet Jesus is pressing upon us that service is more about relationship than responsibility. It is more about a full heart than a full schedule. It's more about our presence than our presents. The most critical aspect of service is the way that it changes us. It shapes our motives, retrains our minds, and redirects our hearts. It moves us to a posture of humility. The better part of

20   Luke 10:38

21   Luke 22:31

22   Acts 9:4

serving, the part that outlasts the immediate results, is not focused on what serving accomplishes but about who we become through our service. And the growth we experience, the kind that matters most, is not the growth of our ministries or our volunteer numbers but rather the personal growth that takes place within our hearts when we commit ourselves to service.

The Good Portion

Martha was in the kitchen. Mary was in the living room. Martha was serving. Mary was worshipping. And Jesus determined that Mary chose "what is better" or "the good portion" (ESV). The "good portion" is fitting terminology since Martha was busying herself in the kitchen, preparing the food. She was dicing, chopping, and kneading, determined to serve all her guests a generous portion. I suspect that Jesus would've ended up with the biggest portion if Martha were the one heaping the food onto the plates. Yet Jesus redefines the good portion to mean something else entirely.

The good portion is not baking in the oven, nor is it about to be plated. The good portion is not tangible, nor can it be earned through service. Mary, who was completely removed from the area of food service, is the sister associated with the good portion because she chooses Jesus. And this is not the only instance in Scripture where Jesus parallels Himself with nourishment. John 6:27 says, "Do not work for food that spoils, but for food that endures to eternal life, which the Son of Man will give you." A few verses later, "Jesus declared, 'I am the bread of life. He who comes to me will never go hungry, and he who believes in me will never be thirsty'" (John 6:35). The parallel Jesus provides is clear. Martha has concerned herself with temporary sustenance, bread that will be consumed. Mary has chosen the bread of life.

Here is where the story becomes complicated because initially it appears that Martha is getting knocked for her work. If it weren't for

Martha, no one would have dinner. But Martha was drowning in her work. She would clearly fit the mold of a modern day workaholic. She had tunnel vision about all she had to do, causing stress and anxiety to rise up within her. It is vital to grasp that Jesus is not reprimanding Martha's hard work. Nor is He condemning her service. He is instead redirecting her gaze. The kitchen service is important, but it is secondary. We can have Martha's hands, but first we need Mary's heart. Jesus is offering her an out. He is reassuring her that there is a better way, the good portion. But it is not tangible. It involves trust. It also involves surrender. And it involves sitting.

Be Present

Selwyn Hughes sums it up well. "Life works better when we know how to glance at things but gaze at God. Seeing Him clearly will enable us to see all other things clearly."[23] With the brief snapshot we have of Martha, I can surmise her disposition that day. She was most likely a case of "I'm too busy for you." You know the type. You are standing with someone, fully engaged in a conversation, but his or her mind is elsewhere, thinking about the grocery list, dinner plans, what time he or she is picking up the kids. He or she checks his or her phone, looks at his or her watch. He or she is a participant in your conversation physically but not mentally.

I catch myself doing this at church on a regular basis. I mentally check off lists as I move through the church corridors. Tell the ushers when to take offering. Make sure the greeters are handing out the newsletters. Remind the worship team to go on stage at quarter of nine. I'm power walking, clearly on a mission, and then someone stops me. "How are your parents? What is your sister doing these days? Are you dating anyone?" And I must resist the temptation to

---

23   Joanna Weaver, *Having a Mary Heart in a Martha World: Finding Intimacy with God in the Busyness of Life* (Colorado Springs, CO: WaterBrook Press, 2000).

brush them off or mentally check out. I must consciously decide to be present.

I suspect this was Martha's struggle. All of her rushing was for Jesus' sake, but did she even glance His way when He arrived, or was she consumed by her task list? It's easy to be swept into an event with such force that you almost forget its purpose. Perhaps her sister Mary had also been full-throttle in service before Jesus arrived, but once He got there, she stopped. It's as if she said, "That's enough now. It's time to sit and spend time with Jesus." She understood the balance. Strong, powerful Martha doesn't come up for air. Mary relaxes. Martha tenses. One feels the weight of the world on her shoulders; the other realizes that the weight belongs to someone else, and it is best that way.

A Heart Checkup

Jesus is concerned about the health of our hearts, especially concerning our motives in service, but hearts are difficult to pinpoint. Each one is a beating, vital organ, but the way we speak about them hints at more. When we are genuine, we mean it from our heart. When we are nervous, our heart skips a beat, echoing our fluttery anticipation. When we care about something, our heart is invested. And when those tender things called hearts break, it is as if all is shattered and lost, as though we could bend over and pick the tattered shards off the floor. The heart is central to who we are as beings. Our heart has the ability to ache, to smile, to love. There are moments when our heart is simply full, brimming with the utmost of contentment. Other times, our hearts can be dark, murky, and confusing, and they seem to lead us astray.

When my sister was student teaching, there was a boy in her classroom, a first grader, who was concerned about his heart. It all started when he began telling the teacher that Satan was speaking to him. From being exposed to horror movies, he was lacking some of his childhood naivety and innocence.

Midway into the school year, all the kids were notified of an approaching medical checkup. Nothing out of the ordinary …just the basics: weight, height, temperature, blood pressure, and heartbeat. Upon hearing this, the boy went up to the teacher and said, panicked, "I can't let the doctor listen to my heart! He'll hear all the bad things in there." He was fearful, worried, that all the bad stuff would be exposed. Fundamentally, he shrunk into the recesses of his thoughts, questioning, "What would happen if they really knew? What if they could hear the ugly murmurs of my heart?"

Beyond the deep concern we felt for this small boy, I wondered how much darkness we allow to linger in our own hearts. We dislike thinking about it, but oftentimes our hearts contradict the outer layer we present to others. We accept compliments outwardly yet spit them out from within. We serve others yet shudder at our shallow intentions. We appear meek, selfless, and humble when truly, in the caverns of our heart, we are consumed by self. Our hearts are fickle. Every once in a while, they rear their ugly heads when we aren't paying close watch. We mostly avoid our hearts and the private truths they convey. Yet every once in a while, we see glimpses of them and look around us, wondering, "If people knew what I was really like, would I still be lovable? Would my heart stand anyone's examination in its sorry state?"

A quiet voices answers, "Yes."

Jesus is unlike what we know or understand as humans. He is more forgiving of our nature and more sympathizing of our poor decisions. Instead, He looks at the heart (1 Samuel 16:7). He is constantly examining it. And He always reassures us that we are welcome company. This is one thing I love about the interaction between Martha and Jesus. Her attitude is horrible. But she demonstrates bold honesty with Jesus. She approaches Him, angry, vulnerable, and heart out of sorts, and that's their starting place. But He would prefer us to come to Him that way than not come at all. Prayers are allowed to look messy. When you read through the book of Psalms, David is incredibly transparent, raw, and honest with his emotions in his prayer life. Comparatively, in the books of Samuel, we could be appalled by some of David's poor decisions and sinful actions. However, Psalms reveals the temperature of his heart. And in response, God claims David as His beloved.

We are about to observe some of the ways to prevent serving from going south—those times when serving starts out positively, but our hearts take a turn for the worst—and learning how to redirect it. Wherever you are, remember that Jesus wants to mend your weary, imperfect heart. As He does so, you will discover that  our God, who is constantly monitoring the rise and fall of each pounding heartbeat, continually welcomes us into His inner circle.

Ways to Care for Our Heart as We Serve

1. Listen to God's Voice

Joanna Weaver wrote, "Nothing is harder to bear than a burden we're not called to carry."[24] What burdens are you carrying that God has not asked you to carry? It's common within the church. Volunteers, who are hard workers and committed to service, see a job that must be done and see no other help. So they step up to the plate, repeatedly,

---

24   Joanna Weaver, *Having a Mary Heart in a Martha World: Finding Intimacy with God in the Busyness of Life* (Colorado Springs, CO: WaterBrook Press, 2000).

until they cannot go any further. I see it in the church all of the time. The church is a hard place to utter the word no. This entire book is a book about saying yes, but God also validates that we say no sometimes in order to accomplish what He calls us to. We are called to fulfill a job and a purpose, but we are not called to fulfill every job and every purpose. I heard a statistic that stated that about 20 percent of the church does 80 percent of the work.[25] It is not difficult to believe.

When I first started working at the church, I headed up a project for a weekend service in which I needed to enlist one hundred volunteers. I did the math in my head. Twenty-five hundred attendees. One hundred volunteers. Easy! I only needed to persuade less than 5 percent of the normal churchgoers to help me. It was my first experience as a recruiter, and boy, was I in for a shock.

After my first go at recruitment, my sign-up sheets were skimpy. I saw that people were not willing to commit or give of their time. What I saw was the detrimental cycle that occurs among many key volunteers within the church. Instead of twenty-five volunteers helping with teardown, twenty-five others helping with setup, and twenty-five others helping with set construction, the same faithful helpers showed up for every area. They showed up, worked hard, and on the way out would ask, "Are you covered for the next event?" and I would sadly admit that I was still short on help. What was aggravating was that I saw my faithful helpers being overworked, but I had no other options. No one else was willing to step in and carry his or her share of the load. This cycle is what leads to burnout and exhaustion within the church.

A few pages after Luke 10, Jesus has a heated dialogue with a Pharisee. He says,

> Woe to you Pharisees, because you give God a tenth
> of your mint, rue and all other kinds of garden herbs,

---

25 Joanna Weaver, *Having a Mary Heart in a Martha World: Finding Intimacy with God in the Busyness of Life* (Colorado Springs, CO: WaterBrook Press, 2000).

but you neglect justice and the love of God. You should have practiced the latter without leaving the former undone. Woe to you Pharisees, because you love the most important seats in the synagogues and greetings in the marketplaces ...Woe to you, because you load people down with burdens they can hardly carry, and you yourselves will not lift one finger to help them. (Luke 11:42–46)

Jesus' message is straightforward. He is questioning those who rush to the front row in church and diligently pay tithes and offerings, yet they refuse to serve. He continues with, "Woe to you experts in the law, because you have taken away the key to knowledge. You yourselves have not entered, and you have hindered those who were entering" (Luke 11:52). Jesus reiterates the exact same message here that He shares in Luke 10. God reveals His fullness to those who serve (Luke 10:22).

What happens when we become like Mary and begin listening to Jesus is that we hear Him instructing us to take on more or to take on less. Andrea, who heads up the elementary area at GT, says, "Jesus isn't asking you to carry the world, but He also isn't asking you to carry nothing." If everyone is willing to carry their share of the work and listen to what God is asking of them, it will help the church to function in a healthy manner and volunteers to serve without reaching the extremes of burnout or apathy.

2. Remember the Good News: You Are Not Jesus

Joanna Weaver, author of the book Having a Mary Heart in a Martha World, writes about a vulnerable time in her ministry when she reached her limit emotionally, spiritually, and physically. She writes,

I'll never forget crying in the darkness one night many years ago. My husband was an associate pastor at a large church, and our lives were incredibly busy. Carrying a double portfolio of music and Christian education meant we worked long hours on project after project, and the size of the church meant there were always people in need. I would go to bed at night worried about the people who had slipped through the cracks—the marriages in trouble, the children in crisis. I worried about all the things I didn't accomplish and should have, about all the things I'd accomplished, but not very well.

I remember clinging to my husband that night and sobbing as he tried to comfort me. "What's wrong, honey?" he asked ...But I couldn't explain. I was completely overwhelmed.

The only thing that came out between sobs was a broken plea, "Tell me the good news," I begged him. "I honestly can't remember ...Tell me the good news."[26]

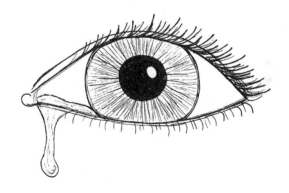

Have you had nights like this? I'm sure most of us have. We become so busy doing things for people and for the church that we forget why. We forget the good news.

The good news is that we are not the ones who are heading up the

26   Joanna Weaver, *Having a Mary Heart in a Martha World: Finding Intimacy with God in the Busyness of Life* (Colorado Springs, CO: WaterBrook Press, 2000).

production. There is a Messiah, and we are not Him. The good news is that we serve a God who conquered death and, consequentially, also conquers all of our shortcomings. God's heart breaks for us when we overdo and outperform ourselves into a state of paralysis. I think He probably wonders how we thought we could do it all by ourselves. In Scripture, He repeatedly persuades us to avoid getting to this place. In Exodus, He says to His people, "What you are doing is not good ... you will only wear yourselves out. The work is too heavy for you; you cannot handle it alone" (Exodus 18:17–18). He consoles those who are tired by beckoning, "Come to me, all you who are weary and burdened, and I will give you rest. Take my yoke upon you and learn from me, for I am gentle and humble in heart, and you will find rest for you souls" (Matthew 11:28–29).

When you start to get the Messiah complex, where you believe you are running the show and are crashing under the weight of it, turn your worries into prayers. It's an extremely simple idea, but it trains your mind to depend on God. Instead of dwelling on your concerns by repeating them in your mind, phrase them as prayers. It is a subtle difference in phrasing but a massive repositioning of the heart. It is the difference between insisting you are in control and manipulating the situations by dwelling on them or offering them up as a concern that you are entrusting into God's control. Galatians 3:3 says, "After beginning with the Spirit, are you now trying to attain your goal by human effort?" The work we are doing is for the Lord, so in the midst of it, He will not desert us.

3. Never Work Alone

Martha must've felt lonesome the day Jesus came to her house. Mary abandoned her, and Jesus seemed to as well. Her load was heavy, and she was the only one to bear it. Have you ever felt like God is in the general vicinity but has abandoned you? His eyes have glanced away. His preoccupations are focused elsewhere. Have you felt like the other members of your church or ministry have left you with all the work? Or like you are the only one who cares? Maybe you feel alone in your leadership role. Or like your loyalty has gone unnoticed or underappreciated. In all of these instances, the burden of loneliness is heavy.

It's nice to believe that once Jesus arrives, Martha's home will be happy, contented, and winsome. Don't you hope that His presence will bolster spirits like a perpetual dose of serotonin? He certainly creates a buzz; however, the joy of His arrival gradually filters through the cracks of distraction and discouragement. These things isolate Martha, creating an emotional wall of loneliness. Eventually her loneliness manifests itself through bitterness. Although the house was most likely full of people, a ready-made community, her service isolated her from the others.

Serving can be a lonely job. When everyone is in the sanctuary and you are in the nursery, changing diapers, loneliness is a familiar companion. When you lead through worship leading, teaching, or preaching, there is a constant separation between you and the rest of the community. As they sit, you stand. As they receive, you give. Most people I know who work at a church rarely sit in the service as a participant. Therefore, it is essential that they find other outlets for spiritual growth.

Growing up in a pastor's family, I am well acquainted with many people who work in the ministry. The most heartbreaking part of seeing ministry up close is hearing the stories of pastors who get derailed, damaging their family, their church, and their calling. And it occurs more often than we'd like to admit. Whether it's an addiction, an affair, or an ominous secret that finally surfaces, it appears among the most unlikely candidates. Steadfast people like Martha who eventually erupt. The people it happens to—the pastors, the leaders, the key volunteers—were not bad people. They were people who started out well with a heart after God and a love for people. How did they end up in the trenches of despair, depression, and failure?

Perhaps loneliness crept in. They felt unaccomplished in the ever-revolving wheels of life in ministry. Without a solid place to turn, these problems are internalized and manifest themselves in unhealthy ways. The new attitude becomes "Lord, don't you care?" with an accusatory finger pointed at God. The lack of a support system leads many healthy people down the road of loneliness. It is heartbreaking to see strong leaders fall apart. When the type-A, always-in-control Marthas of the church internally crash.

Although there is no cure for loneliness, there is the promise of God's presence and provision, even when it is not felt. It reminds me of Jacob in the Bible. After receiving the family inheritance, his brother Esau set out to take his life, and Jacob hightails it out of town. Jacob ends up alone in a desert, disheartened and wandering, a lonely nomad. Yet God approaches him through a dream and reminds him of a promise. When Jacob awakens, he thinks the powerful statement, "Surely the Lord was in this place, and I was not aware of it" (Genesis 28:16). In our lonely times, during our nomadic treks within our solitary service, it can forever be an encouragement to us that the Lord is there, even when we are unaware of it.

4. Remain Faithful

The waiting period is a disheartening state in ministry. It varies in appearance but always involves long spans of what seems to be nothing. For some, it is waiting for new volunteers. Or maybe it is for a strong leader to rise up who can rally a particular area so you can move into a new one. For others, it is diligently pouring into a ministry like a small group, an urban outreach, or a church service and never seeing growth, resulting in feelings of failure. The waiting period, especially when you are diligent in your service, can be a trying and exhausting time. But don't lose heart.

There is a story in the Bible about a woman who had been hemorrhaging for twelve years. Her body never stopped losing blood, socially confining her and debilitating her every movement and activity. Her pale skin was ragged from years of bleeding, affecting her circulation, heart rate, and energy levels. Her eyes were tired; weariness shadowed her face. The bleeding seemed to flush away any hopes of a normal or hopeful future. She sought medical advice and spent a high price on treatments that continually led to her worsened condition. Although disheartened, she knew that if only she could get close enough to touch Jesus…or even the clothes He was wearing …she would be cured. She was sure of it. When she finally encountered this teacher of the law, radically different, loving, wise, honest, and truthful, her bleeding ceased. Her agony ended. That part of her journey came to a close.

What catches and trips me up about this story is not that this woman had a head-on collision with Jesus but that she suffered for twelve years previously. Twelve years of suffering. In Scripture, we only read this small portion where Jesus says, "Daughter, your faith has healed you. Go in peace and be freed from your suffering."[27] Just like that—her pain, her unanswered prayers, her sorrow—all vanished! But why did Jesus, the almighty God, allow her pain to drag on if it was to ultimately lead to her healing? A year, even two, might have been sufficient. But twelve?!

God's timing baffles me. The timing of the occurrences in our lives, the swirl of activity that takes place in seasons, seeming to have neither rhyme, reason, or rhythm baffles me. Timing can also be beautiful. An unexpected collision with fate. A chance meeting that changes an eventual outcome. In a blink, the timing of a single happening can be pivotal, essentially affecting everything else succeeding it. Amazing and unbelievable things can happen when a collision of unlikely timing occurs. It seems that God works under two streams—one of delay and one of urgency. Sometimes He wants us to wait it out—to stay strong through the months and years and decades of uncomfortable circumstances.

---

27   Mark 5:34

Yet at other times, He comes urgently, practically running, declaring, "Your faith has healed you. Go in peace and be freed from your suffering." And in that moment, the clock hands hit midnight. The clock sings of arrival. Healing and renewal breaks through any previously familiar shackles! And we who were once clock-dwellers, counting the minutes, agonizing, waiting, find that the endurance and the faith it took to make it to the final hour were all orchestrated beautifully by the Master Creator. Timing is a terrifying, tedious balance in which our lives rest.

So what do we do in the midst of the waiting? Joanna Weaver answers,

> Ask God to reveal the next step. As you go through your day, keep asking the Lord, "What is the one thing I need to do next?" Don't let the big picture overwhelm you. Just take the next step as he reveals it—wash one dish, make one phone call, put on your jogging clothes. Then take the next step …and the next.[28]

5. Cling to Community

When Martha was slaving away in the kitchen, she probably heard the laughter of her guests. The happy chatter of those she was entertaining was fueling her aggravation. Scripture describes her as distracted,

---

28   Joanna Weaver, *Having a Mary Heart in a Martha World: Finding Intimacy with God in the Busyness of Life* (Colorado Springs, CO: WaterBrook Press, 2000).

which is the original Greek word of perispao. It means "to be over occupied about a thing; to draw away."[29] Her service was drawing her out of community, and she had no one to cling to until she finally came to Jesus.

Jesus sends the seventy-two workers out two by two for a reason. He understands that we work better with others. It is the same reason why He created marriage because He knew that man should not be alone. It is the primary reason for the church. Community is a crucial, beautiful part of the body of Christ. If you are alone in your service, begin to pray that God will send someone as a helper. It's important for leaders to find other ministry leaders to connect with. If you are worn out, do not deal with it alone. Seek community, and when you find it, cling to it.

If there was a likely candidate for burnout, it would have been Jeremy. His wife, Lucretia, was the coordinator for the children's ministry at Glad Tidings on Saturday nights. She was in her mid-thirties when she suddenly became ill and lost the battle to cancer, leaving behind a husband, three young kids, and many brokenhearted people. But in that traumatic time, instead of burning out, Jeremy stepped into Lucretia's position at the church. In his time of brokenness, he chose to serve, and the community of people who he served with became his family and support. There is beauty in community. The wonderful part about service is that it naturally forms a family of people who share a vision and a purpose, and the most unlikely of people are brought together as a family, forming a community. When Mary shared community with Christ, Spurgeon describes it as follows: "Everything was gone from her but her Lord and the word which He was uttering." [30]Community prevents burnout and enhances the spontaneous adventure of a life chasing the spirit of Christ.

---

29   Thayer and Smith. "Greek Lexicon entry for Perispao". "The NAS New Testament Greek Lexicon". 1999.

30   C. H. Spurgeon, *Spurgeon's Sermons on New Testament Women* (Grand Rapids, MI: Kregel Publications, 1994).

6. Rest Up—Sabbath

Since the beginning of creation, God patterned a cadence for living that He suggested we follow. He worked, labored, and created for six days straight, and then on the seventh day, He rested. He paused. He reflected. He was the first to illustrate a Sabbath. God must have felt that the Sabbath was important. Not only did He incorporate it into the first week of the world, but He also ranked it among one of the top Ten Commandments, instructing, "Remember the Sabbath day by keeping it holy" (Exodus 20:8). Sabbath, in His opinion, was not only to be remembered, but it was also to be kept holy. God indicates that the Sabbath should be untouchable. We shouldn't mess with it. As we order the events and activities of our lives, the Sabbath is a critical piece. In Hebrew, Sabbath is the word shabbat, which means rest[31]. Why would God place such a heavy emphasis on the idea of rest? Is rest the one thing that Jesus is trying to teach Martha, and is intentional rest in fact a form of worship? These are all important questions.

I think that God places emphasis on Sabbath as a means of caring for us. Sabbath, in some ways, is a reminder that we are human. We are fragile. We are not fluid, far-reaching beings. We have a start and an end. And we must diligently care for the time, work, and people allotted to us. The question then becomes, how do we care for what God has bestowed us with if we are moving at a frenzied pace, never discerning where God is and what He is asking of us? We were not meant to give of ourselves tirelessly until we crash and burn. We were built for longevity, for rhythm. Our lives were meant to ebb and flow as we slowly walk the pathways of a life of faith and humble service. God speaks this aspiration over His people in Isaiah 40:31, "They will run and not grow weary, they will walk and not be faint." It is His basic desire for us to persist. As a means toward the goal, He teaches

---

31   Ethan M. Allen, *An Introduction to Hebrew Customs of the Bible* (Lincoln City, OR, 2008).

that the best possible way to achieve this slow and faithful canter is through devotion to Sabbath.

At the heart of the issue sits the gift of time, and Sabbath is the art of using time well. I attended a leadership retreat where pastor and professor Bill Dogterom taught about time. There were a few basic principles he shared. One was this: "There is no such thing as 'time' management. Time is unmanageable. There is only self-management, in time." The good news? "You will have time and life for everything Jesus wants you to do." The bad news? "You will not have time and life for everything Jesus wants you to do, and everything you want to do, and everything everybody else wants you to do."

If this is true, which I believe it is, what is Jesus asking us to do? He is undoubtedly asking us to build a Sabbath into the fabric of our lives. Sabbath is the launching pad. From the time spent in rest, we will be able to discern how to spend the rest of our time in action. It makes sense. It is impossible for us to hear what Jesus desires us to do amidst the clamor in the kitchen. It is not until we intentionally choose to move away from our service long enough to sit with Jesus that we can clearly hear what He is asking of us.

Another lesson that Sabbath teaches us is that our service is more about who we are becoming than what we are doing. Again, Mary and Martha stand as examples. Martha was defined by the work of her hands, but her sister Mary was defined by the words of her Savior. Mary was being called out as the beloved while her sister was allowing her calloused hands to define her calloused heart.

Sabbath is like a foreign country for many of us. It seems like a far-off land, a vacation we wish we could take, a quiet that cannot be heard above all of the noise. Sabbath seems like a non-reality. In a culture saturated by overworked, overcommitted, deadline-driven lives, we are all versions of Martha looking at Mary, thinking, "How can you afford to be sitting at a time like this?" For many of us, I doubt we even understand Sabbath. Do not be fooled into thinking that a Sunday morning spent at church volunteering in the nursery and helping at a potluck for the remainder of the day is a Sabbath. Sabbath is the posture of a soul at rest, but it is also a physical slowing. A Sabbath is a tangible intentionality. The psalmist writes, "Be still and know that I am God" (Psalm 46:10). There is a correlation between knowing God and being still because it is difficult to know God until we are still. We cannot be familiar with God's voice if we are not attuned to hearing Him speak.

Sabbath is a time to listen. It is a time to disconnect and recalibrate. For some of us, disconnecting might be literal, to resist the urge to check e-mail or be readily accessible through technology. If you find yourself attached to your phone and computer, I encourage you to select a time slot where you power down. Choose to spend time with Jesus and with those you love without a screen battling for your attention.

Back to my own retreat in the mountains, stepping back was quite literal for me. I knew it was necessary to completely isolate myself for a time until my soul could recuperate and find healing. I sought out alone time with God, not to produce a result, but because my soul needed to slowly recalibrate. My decision to retreat was pivotal in helping me to get back on track. I returned feeling that the strength that had fled from my harried life had been replenished.

If the Sabbath is a new habit for you, I assure you that it will not feel natural. The quiet is unusual. The quiet is uncomfortable. It's weird and countercultural. But the quiet is vital to a healthy spiritual life. It is essential to the life of a servant. The Lord we serve is not a slave master, working us until we are bone-tired and worn. He invites us into a balanced life of work and rest. He wants to take care of us and protect us from destruction.

Q: What are some steps you can take to recalibrate your life?

Mark Driscoll said in a sermon, "If Jesus is last, you'll never get to Him." He continued on to say, "Worship God before you work so that you can worship God in your work." [32]

For many involved in ministry, Sabbath is often not on a Sunday. Sabbath is a time to walk away from the performance, not step into it. As you set out to place priority on a Sabbath in your own life, release yourself from the idea that it looks a specific way. Especially for pastors, the Sabbath might never look like sitting in a service and enjoying prayer time at the altar. It will take on different appearances depending on how you connect with God and which spiritual disciplines you focus on. In my own life, Sabbath is a time of reflection and connection with God. Sometimes it looks like a long walk or a journal entry. My times of rest are a way to manage unhealthy adrenaline and anxiety in my life. A Sabbath does not need to be spent in stoic isolation. A Sabbath can be enjoyed amongst family or friends, but intentionality is what is vital. Many actions are glorifying to God, including intentional relationship building. The difference is that when you start labeling items under the category of Sabbath, they take on new life and meaning. If you plan on eating dinner with your family or your small group, resist the tendency to rush around and play the perfect hostess. Plan out the details earlier in the week. Enjoy the good company. Speak words of kindness. It transforms a simple dinner within a community into an intentional activity built into your Sabbath. I once heard Beth Moore say this about the last supper at a conference, "What was a meal to everyone else was a communion to those who believed."

Learn to build a regular Sabbath into your schedule by setting aside a specific day that takes on a different persona than the others, one that is not bogged down by heavily scheduled responsibilities. Build one day into your week that is slow, steady, and life-giving.

---

32 Mark Driscoll, "Mary and Martha," *Mars Hill Church* (audio blog), September 19, 2010, Luke's Gospel: Investigating the Man Who is God, http://marshill.com/media/luke/mary-and-martha.

The story is told of a migrant South African tribe that regularly went on long marches. Day after day they would tramp the roads. But then, all of a sudden they would stop walking and make camp for a couple days. When asked why they stopped, the tribe explained that they needed the time of rest so that their souls could catch up with them.[33]

Sabbath allows our souls to catch up with our bodies. Jesus is being kind to us and lovingly urges us, as He did with Martha, to take rest and abide in Him so that our work can have more meaning. "If then you are wise, you will show yourself rather as a reservoir than as a canal. For a canal spreads abroad water as it receives it, but a reservoir waits until it is filled before overflowing, and thus communicates without loss to itself, its superabundant water."[34]

Q: What does Sabbath look like for you?

All Hands on Deck

I walked up the aisle, eyes scanning for my seat. I spotted a curly blond head that lifted to reveal a smiling face as I shuffled into my row. I situated my bags for the direct flight to JFK as we exchanged introductions. We chatted easily, and the bright Princeton grad gave me a synopsis

---

33   Joanna Weaver, *Having a Mary Heart in a Martha World: Finding Intimacy with God in the Busyness of Life* (Colorado Springs, CO: WaterBrook Press, 2000).

34   Bernard, *Life and Works of Saint Bernard: Abbot of Clairvaux* (London: John Hodges, 1896).

of her recent trip overseas. It was the final leg of the journey for her and the forty others in her company. She seemed of a different breed than the rest of her rowdy group. She had warm eyes but a wild spirit. The plane began to hum for liftoff, and our conversation quieted. I pulled out my magazine, and she pulled out her booklet of crossword puzzles. That is when I noticed it. My new friend's left arm was amputated at the elbow. I averted my eyes so she wouldn't catch my lingering glance. My mind started racing with questions. Had she been born without a left hand? Or was it more recent, and if so, how had it happened? I wondered what sort of tragedy had occurred.

When the plane landed, everyone started clapping. I thought of my neighbor who didn't have the privilege. She dropped her phone between the seats and struggled to retrieve it with her other arm. We bid our good-byes, but after we parted ways, I could not forget about her and her amputated arm through my entire trip. What gripped me was that she so easily could have been me. She was a young girl who loved exploring. She loved travel, literature, and art.

On the plane, I had been reading a chapter in my book about entitlement. I wondered if she had ever been mad at God about that hand. I am a rotten person, I thought, fixating on such small matters, yet I have both my hands. And even if I didn't, there is still so much to be thankful for. I realized that I needed to reach deeper and see that life is richer than the many superficial things I worry about on a daily basis. Upon landing at my destination, I assumed I would be spending much of that trip working on the SERVE book. It turns out that I did not have time to write, but rather my SERVE homework was much more hands-on. As I assisted a friend and her family throughout the week, I was constantly reminding myself, "You have two hands. Do good with them."

Sometimes service looks a lot like my friend who is an amputee. We are wounded and jaded and restricted, but God still wants to use us. We do not always know what to expect going into it, and sometimes we don't even feel like we are capable or emotionally sound enough to do the job. But we are called to do it anyway. In fact, we are most influential in our service when we have a story to tell that is thick with loss and wounds. Our love is boundlessly accentuated through our pain and God's redemption of it. Brennan Manning writes, "In love's service only wounded soldiers can serve."[35] God is constantly reminding us of what we have to give, whether it is our hands, words, writing, or labor. Regardless, it always starts from our heart, which is why experiencing growth is essential. Spending time in the living room reminds us that Jesus wants us to come so He can work on our hearts as we bring our presence, obedience, and adoration to Him—along with our thankfulness that He even chose to bother with us at all.

Toward the end of writing this book, I was personally faced with a serious decision in my own life. As I contemplated and prayed, I found Isaiah 41:8–10 that says,

> But you, O Israel, my servant, Jacob, whom I have chosen, you descendants of Abraham my friend, I took you from the ends of the earth, from its farthest corners I called you. I said, "You are my servant"; I have chosen you and have not rejected you. So do not fear, for I am with you; do not be dismayed, for I am your God. I will strengthen you and help you; I will uphold you with my righteous right hand.

In response, I wrote these words in my journal, "As my friend Carlos said, it is hard to make the decision, but I'm thankful for the ability to choose. God's words in Isaiah have breathed hope into me this morning. I have so much growth and internal strength to gain, but You have shown Yourself faithful. And maybe that's the lesson— that regardless of my wavering, You do not. You are not fickle like I

---

35   Brennan Manning, *Abba's Child: The Cry of the Heart for Intimate Belonging* (Colorado Springs, CO: NavPress, 2002).

am. You are a tower. I am a breeze. You pour promises over us, and I question their truthfulness. I want to see them immediately, but You allow for these desert places to teach us ...You ask us to be servants, and then You reveal Yourself only to those who humble themselves to that lowly position. One hundred pages into this idea of service— it is still difficult to grasp, to believe, to live, but I am experiencing growth. My heart is learning. Thank You for Your faithfulness and for choosing me."

God is extending an invitation to all of us. It is this: "Serve people. Love people. Give to people." It is painted vibrantly through the stories of Luke 10, through the four Gospels, and again in these verses in Isaiah. Those who choose to serve understand God's message of love and, therefore, are donned as His chosen people. If you have two hands or even a heart that is willing to say yes, God invites you to join Him in this adventure of life devoted to service to fulfill the redemptive plan that He has for His people.

Chapter Summary

>> Service is more about relationship than responsibility.

>> Service is more about a full heart than a full calendar.

>> Service is more about our presence than our presents.

>> The growth that matters most is not the growth of our ministries or our volunteer numbers but rather the personal growth that takes place within our hearts when we commit ourselves to service.

>> Jesus neither reprimanded nor condemned Martha's hard work. Instead, he was redirecting her gaze. The kitchen service is important, but it is secondary.

>> We are called to fulfill a job and a purpose, but we are not called to fulfill every job and every purpose.

>> The good news is that we are not the ones who are heading up the production. There is a Messiah, and we are not Him.

» Turn your worries into prayers.

» Although there is no cure for loneliness, there is the promise of God's presence and provision, even when it is not felt.

» Jesus sent the seventy-two workers out two by two for a reason. He understands that we work better with others.

» The wonderful part about service is that it naturally forms a family of people who share a vision and a purpose, and the most unlikely of people are brought together as a family, forming a community.

» Community prevents burnout and enhances the spontaneous adventure of a life chasing the Spirit of Christ.

» We were not meant to give of ourselves tirelessly until we crash and burn. We were built for longevity and rhythm.

» There is a correlation between knowing God and being still because it is difficult to know God until we are still.

» We cannot be familiar with God's voice if we are not attuned to hearing Him speak.

» Quiet is vital to a healthy spiritual life; it is essential to the life of a servant.

» Jesus lovingly urges us, as he did with Martha, to take rest and abide in Him so our work can have more meaning.

Questions

» Are you carrying too much weight? Too many burdens? Too busy a schedule? If so, what must you say no to right now?

» Have you ever entertained a "Messiah complex?"

» If you feel alone in your service to God, what can you do to change that?

» What are some steps you can take to recalibrate your life?

» What does your Sabbath look like? If you can't answer this question, what decisions must you make in order to answer it?